Prescriptions & Prayers

Healing From Childhood Trauma and Guidance

for First-Generation Minority Medical Students

Mujidat,

I won't be here in Portland today without you, Queen. Thank you for being LOVE.

-gg

GINA GUILLAUME, MD

Junkanoo Publications is a professional publishing division of Junk@Noo Consulting LLC.
www.junkanoopublications.com
Valdosta, GA

Editor:
Margo Thomas Consulting

ISBN: 979-8-9859839-8-2 (Paperback)

The stories and events in this book are true, real-life events accounted for by Dr. Gina Guillaume. Still, to protect the privacy of certain individuals some names have been changed.

The stories and events in this book are true, real-life events accounted for by Dr. Gina Guillaume. Still, to protect the privacy of certain individuals some names have been changed.

Table of Contents

Preface

There is a perpetual war against our youth and young adults worldwide. Brilliant, bold, beautiful youth are facing emotional, physical, and sexual abuse; peer pressure; increasing gun violence; and the abortion of their dreams because of harsh upbringings and toxic environments. I know firsthand the experience of deep childhood abuse coupled with the conditions of poverty and discrimination. These are all strategic plots of a real enemy who seeks to influence God's children to give up on their dreams and lay down their purpose in life due to fear, shame, doubt, low self-esteem, and a deep longing to fit in.

Believe me, based on what you will read throughout this book, I was the least likely to live beyond the territories of my high-crime neighborhood where teenage pregnancy was expected, burglaries were a rite of passage, drugs were sold like candy, and few people went on to higher education—and if they did, it was typically a result of being good at sports.

Doctors rarely came out of my island of Grand Bahama in The Bahamas with a population of now 40,000 people, and doctors certainly were not expected to come out of my tiny town of Eight Mile Rock (aka 'The Rocks'), whose population was 4,000, and more specifically, no doctor emerged from my settlement of Jones Town, with less than one thousand people.

Nonetheless, the God whom I believed in from a young age made what seemed to be impossible, possible. For the first time, in this memoir, I am sharing, in detail, the specifics of my childhood trauma, its effects on my life, and how my faith in Jesus Christ gave me the courage and stamina necessary to follow my dream of becoming a medical doctor.

The environment that raised me, along with the experiences I went through as a child helped to shape the woman I am today. Though bumpy and borderline caustic, each misstep led me to a beautiful journey of self-discovery and purpose. Take it from firsthand experiences, you do not have to be a statistic. No matter where and how you started - with faith, tenacity, and the right community you can dare to pursue your dreams, no matter how grand they are. I hope this book will speak to your soul, ignite your passion to pursue and achieve your dreams, and never give up hope, no matter your circumstances.

Dedication

I dedicate this book to my best friend of 17 years, Ebony Harris, Esq. You are living proof that big dreams can come true, despite small beginnings. Thank you for believing in me, for supporting my advancement, and for pushing me to be my best self. You are a fitting example of a true friend. You and I became a doctor and an attorney, respectively, from the ground up with a faithful Jesus by our side. May our testimonies motivate little boys and girls from disadvantaged upbringings to achieve beyond their circumstances.

Chapter I

Growing Up In
"The Rocks"

Figure 1 *- Gina in her Martin Town Primary School uniform on a 5th-grade field trip in The Bahamas*

I t amazes me how much God can make out of so little. I grew up in the 1990s on the island of Grand Bahama, in The Bahamas with a population of about 24,000 people at the time. During my childhood, The Bahamas planted roots of hope and hospitality deep within my soul by teaching me how to be grounded and grateful all at once. Our neighbors knew us by name and had full permission to "snatch us" if we were misbehaving in public.

The Bahamas is collectively known as an archipelago of 700 islands and cays, including Grand Bahama, one of its northernmost islands. Its main city, Freeport, was centrally located, while Eight Mile Rock (EMR), was toward the western end of the island, further divided into various towns.

Our small town of Jones Town, in Eight Mile Rock, was full of adventure. There was never a dull moment in the green and white 2-bedroom, 1 ½ bath wooden house we called home. My dad cultivated the Caribbean soil and grew various trees and shrubs that decorated our yard with grace. A large mango tree stood in front of our house providing shade for visitors and juicy yellow-colored fruit during the season. Green banana trees were positioned to the far right of the mango tree. My dad boiled and ate bananas like clockwork. A soursop tree shaded the right of our house. My mother would grind the soursop fruit into a creamy juice cocktail that *blessed our lives*. Behind the house grew a sugar apple and a sea grape tree and I tied two pieces of rope around these trees to create a swing. Bush teas like cerasee, moringa, and fever grass, which lined the periphery of our yard were used by my parents to treat all ailments. Simply put, The Bahamas was the country where God lived.

My hometown was indeed lively. Our next-door neighbors to the left of our house were Jamaican and lived in a beautiful cream and black brick home where the scent of curry permeated our atmosphere. In front of us, facing the road, was a blue and white shanty-style house that was occupied by various people over the years. The most memorable was a drug dealer, named Horis who brought so much life to our town. Horis drove around playing his music very loud, so loud you could hear the bass of his 90s reggae music as the rhythm pulsated through your body. As such, our town was always festive because of him, and his music. Horis also had a strange affinity for speed. Whenever he hopped into his car, he slammed his feet on the gas pedal and seemingly flew down the street into oblivion

— like magic, he disappeared as soon as his car door closed.

Horis was gone a lot, handling his business, or catching up with female friends, I presumed. Although he only occupied the blue and white house for a few months, we became accustomed to his routine. When Horis moved out and left our neighborhood, the atmosphere was never quite the same without the sound of his high-powered speaker system and screeching car.

Nonetheless, I had a personal love for adventure as a child. I roamed the yard playing with my siblings and neighborhood friends. My favorite games were Hopscotch, Red light-Green light-1-2-3, Hide and Seek, and childhood hand games, such as Slide, Numbers, and Miss Mary Mac. Our elementary schools and churches also provided summer activities that kept me intrigued such as the Girl's Brigade in Sea Grape, a nearby town where we practiced marching in coordinated lines in preparation for community festivals. My favorite summer adventure though, was a week-long summer camp sponsored by the Salvation Army. We got up at 5 a.m. to interact with neighbors in our assigned age group and waited on the yellow school bus to pick us up and take us to town. At summer camp, we participated in arts and crafts, skating, singing, water sports, swimming and other activities. Being a kid in Jones Town, Eight Mile Rock was awesome! We didn't have much, but we had the joy of life and enjoyed what God put in our hands.

Then there was Youth Group, also known as 'Gwoup Jen' in the Haitian Catholic Church. Church was not an option growing up— our parents ensured we attended mass every Sunday. During the week, we would go to the youth group led by Shauna Taylor, Acel, and eventually, Ms. Lorena, our beloved youth leaders in the Haitian Catholic Church. Our dearly loved bus drivers, the late Odiles Williams and Fwé Bazile would alternate picking up a group of 10-15 of us from each of the towns in Eight Mile Rock on Thursday evenings—God bless their soul. Our 'gwoup jen' was a lot! In our group were boisterous comedians who were also class clowns that kept the whole bus laughing the entire ride. There were stylish *'gyals'* who typically *'dressed to kill'*, 'playas' who were 'hitting on all the gyals', and me, the 'quiet observer' who was deeply into her books.

It did not end there. I often walked to the bay in my hometown of Eight Mile Rock, Grand Bahama, to stare at its halo—a sun reflected on the waters like the glow of jewels, complemented by the clearest, most turquoise ocean the eye has ever beheld. Rocks and sand scattered across our pristine beaches accompanied by the purest and most colorful seashells that decorated the terrain like royalty. Truly, it was "Better in The Bahamas".

Most definitely, we were always surrounded by hospitality, music, togetherness, beauty, and great food, including my favorite dish, a whole fried fish. All 700 islands and cays making up The Bahamas slightly whisper a brilliance that grips visitors with just one look. Most people who visit the islands of The Bahamas find it difficult to leave. Because of my experience with this beauty, I can deeply appreciate the simplest things in life.

Growing up, it was often said that our island was a "Christian Nation" and truly these humble beginnings brought me face-to-face with Jesus. The Bahamas gave me the gift of Christ before I knew I needed Him and for this firm foundation, I am indebted to my upbringing in The Bahamas.

Equally as true, I was raised in one of the poorer settlements of Jones Town, in Eight Mile Rock (affectionately known as 'The Rocks'), where it was too common for our insect-infested shanty-styled house to be burglarized, even while occupied. In fact, my parents never dared to leave our home unattended for fear of an inevitable break-in. Many of our neighbors sold and smoked marijuana (weed) and it was common to see a joint being rolled or sold at different times of the day.

Both of my parents were born in Haiti. For my dad, who was born in Port-de-Paix, and my mom who is from St. Louis Du Nord, poverty was ingrained in them from birth. My mother with an 8th-grade education and my father with a 5th-grade education immigrated illegally to The Bahamas separately and met on the island.

I often wondered what kind of love connection two foreigners could have back in the 1970s in a place so far away from home, but, my parents met and birthed four beautiful children. I am the third of these four children with an older sister and an older and younger brother.

My parents risked it all to brave cold and unfamiliar waters in a boat for a chance to live above the scarcity that was laid out for them from conception. While Haiti is indeed the poorest country in the Western Hemisphere, I do not think my parents were aware of the fierce discrimination that awaited them in The

Bahamas. It is an understatement that there is tension between "Bahamian-born" vs. "Haitian-born" Bahamians. My family was often reminded that we did not belong and that we should go back to our country. It was believed that access to jobs, opportunities, and success was reserved solely for the "true" Bahamian people. To a young girl, the message was clear, we simply did not belong in The Bahamas.

Haitians, Bahamians, and Africans were all from one land, one continent, and one region before the world at large intentionally and successfully divided us. Eventually, I began leaving my community to travel the world, where I was struck by the profound depths of marginalization that people of African descent carry, both in mindset and in practice. We learned in Social Studies classes that the Caribbean was, in fact, originally inhabited by the Arawaks, Caribs, Lucayans, etc., who were the Aboriginal natives forcefully enslaved by Christopher Columbus when he 'discovered' The Bahamas in 1492. Later, we discovered how colonial Europeans subjected the continent of Africa to slavery. They captured African families, piled them in ships, and sailed them across the Atlantic Ocean on the treacherous journey known as the Middle Passage where many slaves died and the ones who survived were scattered throughout what is known as the "New World" (the Caribbean and the Americas).

Yet, I was often reminded by our Bahamian neighbors that my family was different. I was teased frequently because of my last name. Kids accused me and my family of practicing voodoo. We were called, "Ugly" and "Stink", by some neighbors when my mother refused to give away her merchandise for credit. I remember being told to "Carry my Haitian A$$" when my peers got upset with me. You name it, my siblings and I experienced it. The discrimination of Haitians also followed us into the school system as it was frowned upon to speak Creole in public places. Peers sometimes referred to us as "Stank or Ogley Hi-tians" in the thickest Bahamian accent. In the political environment, like clockwork, Haitians were deported, and new laws resurrected like a sunrise to crack down on the *"infestation"* of Haitians in Bahamian land. Still, somehow, my parents found a way to make it work.

I understand that laws were created for a reason, and they keep order, but I draw the line when we start looking down on others based on where they were born. Though tried and tested with economic hardship and political unrest, I still am hopeful of the spirit of

The Bahamas to illustrate peace and justice, through love and unity. Regardless of where we were born, I still believe that Black people can accomplish more justice and order by working together rather than fighting against each other.

Nobody can explain hate, but hate is what I experienced from an early age. Perhaps, this is why I have a heart for underserved and marginalized communities despite eventually becoming Dr. Guillaume. It is because I know what it felt like to be discriminated against before my character spoke for me.

Dad

My dad, dis-affectionately known as 'Mr. Baba', was a barber by trade, who worked out of a room in our home, adjacent to our living room. With precision, my father operated his business with a pair of scissors and a razor blade from 7:00 in the morning to 9:00 at night. It was a blessing that my dad worked from home, but his presence sometimes felt aloof because he worked so frequently. Dad was a brave man. He shaped my impression of what it meant to be a man and the kind of man I should marry—secure, confident, strong, protective, and a provider. He commanded respect inside and outside of our home. Everyone knew who he was and equally how crazy he was. "Mr. Baba don't play, boy!" chimed many of our neighbors. Friends knew not to come over after a certain time. Boys knew not to call at all or only call when I sent them a text message that the coast was clear. Our neighbors trod lightly around my father because they knew at any moment he could 'snap'.

While I appreciated his strength, my dad was also cruel. He barely smiled and found very few things amusing except Monday Night Raw. The WWE wrestling matches kept him glued to the television with his fists raised and his voice shouting in Creole for his favorite wrestlers. "Ba *yo konsa, konsa!*" (Translated: *Give it to them like that! Just like that!*), he yelled at the screen. He monitored the people we associated with and was not afraid to interject how he felt about things that seemed to distract his children. For instance, I clearly remember one day when my big brother and the neighborhood boys were playing basketball in the front yard. In those days, we cut the center out of a crate or bucket, nailed it to a tree or post, and turned it into a basketball "hoop".

During one of my older brother's usual afterschool games of "Buckets" in our front yard, he got into a physical fight with Booboo, one of the neighborhood boys over a flagrant foul. The air was thick and of course, everyone surrounded my brother and Booboo, in true Caribbean fashion in audible support to "Fight! Fight! Fight!". They began to exchange expletives about each other's "Ma" (Bahamian term for mother). Then, they began to fight as the crowd cheered them on. After the steam died down and my brother left the fight bruised, my dad got involved. He not only broke up the fight, but he also got on his ladder with a hammer in his hand and dismantled the crate used as the basketball hoop. This day was the last time an afterschool game of Buckets was played in our front yard and the last I ever recall seeing Booboo around our home.

With a short stature of 5' 2" my dad instilled fear into our household and for most of my childhood I feared him more than I knew. From what my mother told me, well into my twenties, my father was the child of his father's mistress. It was unknown how many siblings my father truly had, but my mother revealed that he grew up with the wife of his dad and was often mistreated by his family because my dad was considered an "outside child". Therefore, my father jumped at the opportunity to leave Haiti at the age of twenty, along with all of the belongings he worked for as a farmer. He hopped on a boat with his comrades and landed in The Bahamas, first living on the islands of Abaco, then New Providence, and eventually moving to Grand Bahama Island where he settled illegally.

My father was already living in The Bahamas when the country celebrated its independence from Great Britain in 1973, though he was not recognized yet as a citizen. I would later ask him why he never settled in America instead, but I was usually met with the response, "It is what it is". My father was truly honored that his legacy would be raising children of virtue rather than pursuing prosperity. I also learned that my father migrated to The Bahamas in the 1960s, which coincided with the Civil Rights Movement in America, a time-period where Jim Crow laws would have barred him from entering businesses through front doors, forced him to sit at the back of buses, and reduced him to the "Colored" section of every water fountain, restroom, school, and the like. My father was a proud Haitian man, so it was no wonder America was not an option for him or his family at that time.

Mom

Then there was my mother, who was affectionately called "Mammy," by the masses. There are not enough documented synonyms for "strong" that would capture my mother's essence. She was a hustler, a chef, a seamstress, a counselor, a comedian, an entrepreneur, a nurturer, a dancer, and everything a man could ever want in a wife.

My mom ran a 24-hour shop out of our home where she sold Haitian peanut cakes, cigarettes, cigars, sodas, alcohol, and other items to our neighbors. Because she operated her business from our home, she woke up late at night if customers knocked at her bedroom window. This was her opportunity to make extra money 24 hours a day, 7 days a week. My siblings and I helped to sell my mom's merchandise when we were home from school. Watching my mother practically work herself to the ground to provide for others introduced me to the concept of selfless love and sacrifice. Whether this was healthy love and sacrifice is a story for another time. Nevertheless, I cannot thank my mom enough for her sacrifices.

One of my favorite pastimes growing up was accompanying mammy to the marketplace in downtown Freeport to shop for her business. The drive to Freeport was a 15-minute bus ride from the Rocks. Our public bus service comprised mostly of small-sized vans that fit approximately fifteen people in total. There were no designated bus stops in the early 90s. To signal that we were waiting on the bus, mammy and I stood outside and waved our hands like we had touched a piping hot stove.

Once inside the bus, we opened a window to let the cool breeze in. Heaven forbid you were seated next to a neighbor who forgot to wear deodorant that day. Our bus driver typically kept the radio on 100 Jamz or ZNS News Network, our local radio stations, where we were able to catch up on the latest music and news happening around the island. As we got close to our destination, mom would yell "Bus stop" signaling to our bus driver to stop at our destination. I was ecstatic to arrive downtown with mammy as she cracked open her roll of quarters to pay the bus driver a dollar for herself and fifty cents, the child's rate for me.

Our first stop was usually to the marketplace located in the International Bazaar (later moved to the downtown location), where merchants sold home-grown fruits and vegetables in an array of containers. Among this produce were Caribbean green bananas, coconuts, mangoes, soursop, meliton (Haitian term for chayote), and Bahamian treats of coconut tart, guava duff, potato bread, and the like. Our favorite stall belonged to my mother's Haitian friend, Dayan. Dayan, who was the sweetest person gladly gave me treats each time we stopped by her stall. Mammy usually got her vegetables for soup or whatever meal she would lovingly prepare that day.

The next stop was typically to pay the electricity bill at Freeport Power (the only major electric company that supplied the island with power), which was housed in the Port Authority building. For the next stops, we waltzed our way to the local bank to pay the cable bill and to the local phone company, Batelco (later renamed, BTC Bahamas) to pay our phone bill. Our final stop was Winn Dixie for a midday snack of Bahamian-style hot and spicy chicken wings and macaroni salad. I enjoyed watching my mother move through the streets of The Bahamas *like a boss*, confidently handling her household affairs, even in a language that was not her own. She seemed to own the streets and taught us to do the same. She handled her business with excellence, joy, and skill.

Mammy was also directly involved in our education. Though she never owned a car she took the public buses from Eight Mile Rock to downtown Freeport and then walked the remaining 2-3 miles to my high school (Grand Bahama Catholic High) on report card days. She usually asked someone to give her a ride back to the bus stop or simply walked the 2-3 miles to return home by public bus. Yet, she never seemed embarrassed or troubled by this inconvenience. She exhibited confidence, joy, and grace through what some people would deem a "struggle", all while wearing the most fashionable outfits you can imagine.

Truly, Mammy was a "Boss"! On top of paying the bills, picking up report cards, shopping for groceries, and managing her business, she still found time to cook the most scrumptious Haitian food, complete household chores, and attend church, while smiling like she was on a daily vacation (and she looked the part). Mammy loved fashion! She never left our home without looking her best with matching handbags, chic-cut blouses, or dresses. I have a distinct memory of Mammy and me standing in a local Burger King in downtown Freeport when one of my high school classmates walked up to us. She looked at us, then asked, "This ya mummy? She don't look Haitian!" I responded instinctively, "What does a Haitian look like?" Her response was a downplayed statement that she didn't mean it like that. I knew she meant exactly what she said. In The Bahamas, discrimination and assumptions about Haitians were real. Nonetheless, Mammy smiled and shone radiantly, knowing she was beautiful, not just externally, but on the inside as well.

Indeed, the Bahamas was lively, beautiful, and my childhood filled with joy and adventure. Yet, beneath the sunshine and laughter, my upbringing was also marked by deep pain and abuse.

Top of the Class

Figure 2 - *Graduating Valedictorian of Grand Bahama Catholic High School at age 16 (June 2007)*

Subconsciously, I buried my shame with achievements. There is an unwritten code of excellence in a Haitian house where children are simply expected to bring home good grades. I saw the sacrifices my parents made for us daily. My mother and father with 8th grade and 5th grade educations, respectively, both worked nonstop to feed and raise four children. Naturally, I felt it was my duty to bring home star-spangled report cards. I also liked the validation that good grades brought me. People suddenly noticed me when they learned that I got straight A's. Teachers became extremely interested in my success, students respected my foreign last name more, and more conveniently, I could bury my shame.

Yes, I was gifted. For instance, I 'swept away' nearly all of the trophies at my elementary school graduation, receiving awards in various subject matters and earning the coveted Valedictorian title at my primary school in 2001. This victorious moment literally brought me to tears as I relished in the joy of my achievements and the attention my gift attracted.

The achievements continued throughout high school. At the time, we did not have formal junior high schools on Grand Bahama Island. As such, most of our high schools started in the 7th grade and progressed through the 12th grade, or there were all-age schools where students started at kindergarten and progressed through to the 12th grade. So, after I graduated from Martin Town Primary (from grades 1-6), I journeyed the streets of Eight Mile Rock, ready to start high school.

I attended Eight Mile Rock High School (E.M.R.H.S), a public school known as the 'Home of the Bluejays' for my 7th grade year. My uniform was a royal blue pleated skirt, white buttoned shirt, royal blue socks, and matching hair ribbons. You could not talk to us! Chal, we were cute! My big brother was also a 'Brain Box' as Bahamians called it. He graduated Salutatorian of his high school graduating class in 2001. By the time I started high school, the Guillaume name was prized. People knew who I was the moment I said my name. Eight Mile Rock High School was an exciting place. I was comfortable and felt right at home with my peers, teachers, and the best principal ever, Mrs. Sandra Edgecombe. Eight Mile Rock High was also near my home, about a mile walk or a 5-minute drive, which provided a sense of familiarity and security.

The fact that my older brother and sister thrived at Eight Mile Rock High, coupled with my reputation of being Valedictorian of my elementary school class, life at Eight Mile Rock High was pretty sweet. Teachers loved me, my peers and I got along, especially the budding Haitian community whom I ate lunch with regularly, and my grades continued to flourish. At the end of my first year at Eight Mile Rock High, I earned a 4.0 GPA.

Soon, Fadda, my childhood priest, also recognized my gift of doing well in school. He visited my home one afternoon, proposing that my parents allow me to transfer to a private Catholic high school known as the Grand Bahama Catholic High School (G.B.C.H.S), 'Home of the Crusaders' on a full tuition scholarship funded by the Catholic Archdiocese of The Bahamas.

My parents were so excited at this opportunity to send one of their children to a private school 'Up Town' in Freeport, but I was devastated. I was afraid of this 'opportunity' because I had grown so comfortable with my surroundings and the fame I had achieved at Eight Mile Rock High. Starting a new school so far away from my comfort zone meant the possibility of my validation being taken away. I was thriving off the praises of others who knew me as the "Smart Gyal". Additionally, I knew I would not blend in with the 'Rich kids' whose parents could afford this education. I saw myself as just a tall Haitian girl from the ghetto, who got good grades in school.

Nonetheless, my parents agreed that this would be a better opportunity for me and signed me up to start 8th grade at this new school. I spent that summer purchasing new school uniforms, taking entrance exams, and shopping for my new book list. My new uniform consisted of a straight grey skirt with a red vest covering a white buttoned-up shirt with red socks and red hair ribbons to match - I was still cute! I started my new school at the prestigious Grand Bahama Catholic High School in the summer of 2002.

Honestly, I felt like I had died. My transition to Grand Bahama Catholic High was rough, to say the least. Since my parents did not own a car, I had to wake up two hours earlier to get ready and stand outside for the school bus that would take me to my new school (a 40-minute drive) instead of simply walking to Eight Mile Rock High up the street. The Haitian population at Grand Bahama Catholic High was small and lunchtime was not as vivacious as it was at my old school. The only person I knew was a pretty boy from my church who lit up a room with his personality. He was a popular kid who sat next to me on the school bus, but was either hanging out with his friends or chasing girls. Not only that, I also learned that I did not score high on the entrance exam, so I was placed in a second-tier class.

My classmates were considered 'bougie' and the teachers who were slightly stuffy, did not have a clue who I was. Indeed, I was not in the Rocks anymore, and the unfamiliarity drove me nuts. I cried often during that first year at Grand Bahama Catholic High. Still, I continued to pray to God to help me. My priest had given me a "Daily Bread" devotional, which I began to read when I started my new school. I read a passage every morning before I left home to wait on the school bus. One morning, around the 9th grade, I made a bet with God while reading through my daily devotional time. Essentially, I asked God if He continued to bless my grades, I would remain a virgin until I was married. As silly as it sounds, it felt like a fair trade to me. After all, my grades were where I found my self-worth and it was how I covered my shame. Plus, purity was stressed at my church anyway.

I performed well enough in the 8th grade and was promoted to the set-one class for 'Gifted' students in the 9th grade. Some of my classmates did not appreciate that I outshined them and on occasion, some of the girls whispered under their breath about my performance. I remember, after I aced a physics test that most of the class failed, one of the girls in my class took my graded paper away from me and demanded that the teacher recheck my answers for errors. To her dismay, there were no errors. I understood all too well when God is blessing you, not everyone will be excited for you, regardless of your age.

The fact that I was so tall also did not help. I always stood taller than the rest of the girls and boys in my class, which added to my already low self-esteem. I struggled to see myself as pretty in high school especially since the boys in my class were typically attracted to lighter-skinned girls with long, curly 'good hair' and were not interested in me. I was tall, dark-skinned, with thick 'African rooted' coils. I often asked my mother to straighten my hair with a relaxer so that I could fit in with the rest of the girls in my class, and ultimately feel pretty.

One day, while in English class, two boys sitting in front of me were having a conversation. One of them was a popular, tall, and handsome guy whom many of the girls drooled over. He said to the other boy, "It usually be the ugly girls who are the nicest ones." The other boy responded, "Like who, Bey?". The popular boy turned his eyes in my direction as if to indirectly signal me out. I received the message—loud and clear. This further added to my lack of self-worth because although the boys in my class thought I was nice; they also did not find me attractive.

Needless to say, attending Grand Bahama Catholic High School was tough, but it taught me endurance. I continued to perform well in school and eventually built relationships with my teachers, who were not so stuffy after all. In fact, my Mathematics teacher from India, Mr. Anthony, helped me to pass a standardized exam in the Bahamas with flying colors because of his exceptional tutoring skills and a secret gift of comedy. Another teacher Mrs. Francis brought Biology to life with her vivid and creative examples that made the material stick all while speaking in the most calm and gracious voice you ever heard. Still, one of the greats was my British English teacher Mrs. Evans, whose accent was melodious and who also knew how to captivate us with written and spoken words. With confidence, my love and skill for writing were shaped by Mrs. Evans. Grand Bahama Catholic High was not Eight Mile Rock High. I was stretched, and the opportunities were, in fact, more profound. Throughout the latter half of high school, I joined several extra-curricular groups, including a science club known as "Battle of the Brains", an all-girls community outreach club sponsored by Alpha Kappa Alpha (AKA) Sorority known as "20-pearls", and I even joined a hiking club known as the Governor General's Youth Award (GGYA). I was also blessed with the opportunity to serve as the Student Council President during my senior year, where my leadership skills grew.

Nonetheless, the heightened discrimination among students and even staff members continued. There was one incident when I wore a t-shirt with the Haitian flag on one of our rare "dress-up" days. Some of my peers teased me about my clothing, using the infamous saying, "Carry ya Haitian self". While I was running for the Student Council President position, these same students were encouraging others not to vote for me because of this reason. One afternoon during my presidency, I was invited into the principal's office where I was asked to step down and give the position to a more qualified team member because I did not have a good rapport with the faculty and my ideas catered too much to the student body.

Discrimination, even among Black people was real for me growing up. I was often reminded that some people intentionally oppress you based on your cultural background, and some will even go as far as reducing your value in an attempt to increase theirs.

Despite this, Catholic High School exposed me to extracurricular activities and dynamic experiences I would have missed at Eight Mile Rock High. I eventually graduated as the Valedictorian of my high school once again and gained the notoriety my soul desperately longed for. Here I was, at age 16, showcased in our local newspaper, respected by many on the island, yet still buried in shame. If I gained nothing else, I learned how to stay strong and push through, even in the face of adversity. Unfortunately, high school is also where the fruits of my unaddressed pain started to manifest in real time.

So where did this shame come from? What exactly was this unaddressed pain that crept into my life so boldly? Was it simply the way Haitians were mocked in The Bahamas? Was it my height—or the sting of being called ugly by my high school classmate? Indeed, there was a deeper level of pain that happened years earlier in my childhood. Long before I had the language to name it, an unspoken wound took root. I buried it, but it taunted me—giving shame a powerful voice that echoed for years.

I. Lessons

◆ Discover what you are good at early and develop those skills through competitions, practice, and attending relevant events/conferences.

◆ Look for ways to get scholarships in courses and activities you are excelling in.

◆ Surround yourself with positive people who will keep you accountable and out of trouble.

◆ Keep busy with extracurricular activities that will keep you out of trouble.

◆ God does not make mistakes. Where you were born, the family you were born into, and where you were raised, all serve a purpose.

◆ Your parents have their own set of traumas they need to overcome. Unfortunately, they can only give you what they know to give. If they were not taught a different way, they cannot give you differently.

- Having a mentor (teacher, coach, family member, church leader, etc.) while living in poverty is paramount to your success.
- Develop a relationship with God early and pray to him often about your dreams.
- Find the beauty in your environment, even if it does not match up with your dreams...yet.

Chapter II

All the Way Up - Traumatized

I was about seven years old when it began. I was molested by three different men who were well-known family friends in my neighborhood. Each instance occurred at the blue and white shanti-house adjacent to our home. For seven years, it was occupied by various people, including a family, a tailor, and a drug dealer. Later, it remained vacant. During Hurricane Frances and Gene, a vicious duo of back-to-back hurricanes in 2004, I watched from a peephole in our house as the fierce winds crumbled the blue and white house from ceiling to floor. Although the building physically disintegrated before my eyes, the traumatic memories from that building did not. The memories were very much alive and would eventually manifest throughout my life, over, and over again.

The first time I experienced sexual activity in that blue and white house was at the age of seven while I was in the 3rd grade. Every morning, I played with my friend Candy and her brother Spa in the blue and white house, which, at the time was occupied by their family. We played Hide and Seek, exchanged our toys, and ran around the yard like we owned it. One morning I went to visit Candy and Spa, but they were still asleep. I opted to return when everybody was awake, but their father Dejean encouraged me to stay. He was watching a movie that I found intriguing, so naturally I went inside to wait for my friends to wake up.

Dejean's wife was not in the living room as she was also still asleep. It was just me and Dejean. He was lying on the couch under a sheet and asked me to join him to get cozy. I did not think anything of it and moved over to the couch to watch the movie with him. In an instant, Dejean pulled me under the covers, unzipped his pants, rested his private parts between my legs, and held me tight. I was confused, afraid, shocked, and numb. He did not penetrate me but instead cuddled his naked body next to my three-foot frame. At the time, I was too numb to move, too ashamed to talk, and too young to process what was actually happening to me. When he heard his children moving about, he quickly pushed me aside on the floor and returned to normal under his sheets, like nothing happened. I told my friends that I was not interested in playing that day and silently went back home, pretending like nothing happened. I had yet to understand what sex was, but in my mind, something unnatural had just happened to me.

Since this occurred with an older man whom I trusted, I brushed it off and held it in, assuming this was common and appropriate behavior. Accordingly, I kept going over to play with my friends. Dejean was up bright and early to greet me smiling like I was his daughter. It is painful to recollect, but Dejean performed this sexual act with me on multiple occasions that year. I assumed this was how men showed their affection to little girls. It was not until the 6th grade when I started to learn about sex from a beloved teacher that I understood what happened to me was wrong and that I was taken advantage of. Still, I told no one.

Years later, during my sophomore year in college, Dejean visited my parents. They were seated in our backyard. I was hesitant to go outside to greet him. I kept what he did to me a secret for so long, but it wasn't a day that I didn't remember what happened. I finally went outside and pasted a fake smile on my face as I greeted Dejean. I reached for a 'church hug' and was baffled when he whispered, "Remember how much fun we used to have in that old house?" *God, I could have killed him! What in the F*%\$# was inside this monster? How the F\$&# could he remind me about the nastiness he did to me when I was a child?* I rushed inside the house, headed straight to the bathroom, and sobbed. Dejean died from some illness when I was twenty-four. *No, I did not shed a tear.*

The Dejean family soon relocated to another settlement in the Rocks. The next occupant of the blue and white house was a Haitian tailor who only occupied a portion of the house. The other part of the house where I sometimes played was semi-abandoned. It was there that I had a second sexual encounter with another family friend, Bob. Bob was a dark-skinned Haitian man with the longest goatee I have ever seen. He visited our home twice a month to either get his hair cut by my dad or to eat my mom's home-cooked meals. He jokingly called me his "girlfriend". He always brought me treats and sometimes left money for me. I felt so loved and, oh so spoiled. Bob also gave me piggyback rides in our front yard. In my experience, he was one of the nicest men I knew. He was like my father, only kinder and more comforting.

However, one random summer day, after 3rd grade, while Bob was giving me a piggyback ride outside, he extended the ride, taking me into the old blue and white house facing my home. My parents were at home and my siblings were around doing sibling things. Bob and I had never ventured this far during a game of piggyback ride before. We mostly stayed within a visible distance of my house. However, on this day, he took me into the semi-abandoned portion of the blue and white house, which at midday was unusually quiet. The house was dark with only a sliver of sunlight coming through the side walls of the old wood. I rested my head on Bob's shoulder and enjoyed the serenity as I considered him to be the nicest man I had ever known. Suddenly, Bob re-positioned me from his back, lifted me in front of him, and started to tongue kiss me with all his might. He unzipped his pants and pulled down my underwear and attempted to penetrate me, but his penis could not fit. Again, I felt pain, confusion, numbness, and shock.

This was the second time a man engaged in a sexual encounter with me. After Bob noticed that his penis was going nowhere, he zipped up his pants, put me on the floor, and bent down on one knee to my eye level. He shook a finger in my face, looked me in the eye, and warned me in Creole to never tell anyone about this or he would kill me. He put me on his back again and gave me a piggyback ride all the way home. After that day, Bob was no longer my "boyfriend". He came by less and less until I barely saw him at all. The last I heard of Bob he had moved back to Haiti. Who knows if he is still alive? Perhaps, he passed away. I never told my parents for several reasons: I was afraid of Bob, and I knew my father would kill him. I also wondered what was wrong with me—Was I asking for this? Was I somehow encouraging these men? Who would believe me? Obviously, it was my fault, right? These experiences filled me with shame that I kept allowing men to have "sex" with me at such a young age. Naturally, more confusion ensued and I did what I knew best. I remained silent and pretended like it never happened. Or so I thought.

Then there was Bubba, the tailor who lived in a section of the blue and white house. Bubba was a tall Haitian man with salt and pepper hair. He moved to The Bahamas illegally, like most Haitians in search of a livelihood and financial security. He established his tailoring company in his home while occupying the rest of the house with a kitchen and bedroom. Like many in our community, he took baths in the community outhouse that was shared between him and my family at the time. Growing up, we did not have an electrical heating system, nor a functioning bathroom for the first seven years of my upbringing. My parents and two older siblings took baths in the 'kay benyen' (bathhouse or outhouse), a wooden shack with one door that opened via a latch. We used a pump, which reminds me of a fire hydrant with a lever we pressed up and down to release the water. We then boiled some of the water on the stove, poured the boiling water in a bucket, and carried the bucket to the outhouse to bathe. Next to the outhouse was our toilet house. Simply put, it was an enclosed wooden shack with a deeply dug hole surrounded by cement. The flies and mosquitos in this part of the yard were unmatched.

Bubba was one of the last people in our neighborhood to use the well and outhouse in our backyard to wash. Bubba was also a frequent flyer inside our home. He went to church with us, ate Sunday dinners with us, and sewed for us. He was indeed a trusted family friend. He and my dad were close and often reminisced about the days growing up in Haiti and their current life in The Bahamas. Haitians stuck together in The Bahamas and supported each other through their shared experiences, mostly steeped in trauma.

Occasionally, I hung around the blue and white house to watch Bubba at work. He was a truly talented and very hard-working artist, creating suits from scratch with fabrics I had never seen before, or tailoring school uniforms for the neighborhood children at cheap prices—anything to survive, right? Bubba sometimes made small talk with me, asking about school and discussing my activities for the day.

He was a nice man and relatively soft-spoken. Unfortunately, this soft-spoken man soon resembled Dejean and Bob. One day, as I was snooping around our yard looking for my latest adventure, Bubba who was busy sewing at his desk, noticed me wandering around and invited me into his tailor shop. I looked up at dozens of luxurious clothing hanging from his closet.

While sitting at his sewing machine, he suddenly stopped what he was doing and told me to sit on his lap so that he could teach me how to sew. I walked my way over and sat on his lap. It started quite innocently with him showing me how to line up the cloth at the tip of the sewing machine. His legs were long enough to press the pedal, and I watched in amazement as we pulled the needle into the cloth and created the first stitch of this soon-to-be skirt. Over time, I watched as he pleated school uniforms, hemmed dresses, and created tuxedos. My favorite part was helping him use the sewing machine. It was fun learning how to sew and hanging around Bubba made me feel useful.

Bubba earned my trust. He was not so bad, I thought. In hindsight, I was comfortable hanging around these men because they provided the quality time, words of affirmation, and physical affection that was absent from my father at home. Dad was always working in the barbershop next door providing as best he could for the family. This meant he had little energy and capacity left over to play, speak to, and affectionately love on his children.

During one of my tailor shop visits, I sat on Bubba's lap as I usually did, assisting him with the sewing machine. We had played this game so many times before, but this time seemed different. Suddenly, I felt a weird sensation underneath my hip. It was like the hardness I felt that day with Bob and under the sheets with Dejean. I quickly brushed the thought off and kept sewing as Bubba pressed the pedal of the sewing machine. The hardness of his erection, however, did not go away. Bubba stopped pedaling, reached over me and tilted me across his lap. He started to kiss me with his tongue and feel over my non-existent bosom and hips. Another man was attempting to have "sex" with me. This rubbing and petting lasted for what seemed like the whole afternoon until Bubba was satisfied. I never went back for sewing lessons. Bubba however, continued going to our Haitian Catholic church with us, eating Sunday dinners, taking Sunday communion, and having profound conversations with my dad about Haiti and Bahamian politics. I grew up with daily thoughts and scents of these men and silently carried around the shame of what happened to me, unprocessed and unaddressed.

Note: I dreaded sharing this part of my story, and for decades I remained silent about it. I am sharing the details of my experience of childhood sexual abuse for the first time in this book because I know I am not the only one who went through these atrocities. Ultimately, I believe sharing these significant events can potentially help other young girls and boys who are living in shame and low self-esteem. By being open about this part of my testimony, I hope that it will initiate, for some, a path to healing from childhood trauma. Remember, the way things start for you does not have to define how your life ends. Healing is truly therapeutic, life-sustaining, and a process. See the Appendix for further resources for survivors of childhood sexual abuse.

Confession

Figure 3 - *Gina's first communion ceremony photo at age 10*

I continued through life as if nothing had ever happened to me. Certainly, education was a perfect way to distract myself from these traumatic events. For elementary school, I attended Martin Town Primary, a local public school just a 5-minute walk from my house, led by the great Mrs. Victoria Wright. Our uniform was a yellow button-up shirt underneath a plaid vest, pleated skirt, and a cross necktie to match (see Figure 1). I loved wearing uniforms and looked forward to getting dressed up for school.

Year after year, I brought home report cards with stellar grades and won every spelling bee competition that came my way. My talent was noticed by my illustrious 5th-grade teacher, Mrs. Lily Moxey, who soon became my mentor. Mrs. Moxey encouraged me to keep reading. She walked with excellence and knew how to encourage excellence in her students. She gave me books to read and hosted sleepovers at her house for a group of her primary school students. Mrs. Moxey discussed topics that we were too embarrassed to speak up about at home. She engaged our impressionable minds and helped us to navigate our first menstrual cycles, peer pressures, low self-esteem, and poverty. She saw a true version of me, not who I was pretending to be. In the 6th grade, I became the

Head Girl of my class (leader of all the class prefects), serving as a liaison between my classmates and teachers, and I also graduated as the Valedictorian of my elementary school class.

I learned quickly that I was exceptional at performing great in school, and at a young age, this is exactly where I found most of my self-identity. The better I performed, the more my parents cheered me on, the more my teachers rewarded me, and the better I became at hiding my pain. While in the 3rd grade, I was featured in our local newspaper for meeting with the then Governor General of The Bahamas, Sir Orville Turnquest. From the outside looking in, I was headed places. Yet, at age ten with all the accolades a small town could offer, I was still in pain and felt like I was going nowhere.

At age ten I was also participating in classes for my first communion. My parents raised me and my siblings in church, from the time I could remember. We attended Our Lady of Perpetual Help Haitian Roman Catholic Church under the leadership of the late Father Remy, who was known affectionately as 'Pè Remy' or 'Fadda'. First Holy Communion was a special ceremony for young Catholics. We were enamored with the hope of eating the light wafer and drinking real red wine which represented the body and blood of our Lord, Jesus Christ, respectively. However, this was a process. Preparing for first communion meant attending weekly classes (known as 'Catéchis' in Creole) at a local church leader's home where we were taught about the Bible and the traditions and prayers of the Catholic faith. After 8-12 weeks of classes, the priest tested us individually on what we learned to deem us fit for our first communion. Once the priest gave us a passing grade, we would then participate in our first 'Confession' where we privately met with him to confess all of our sins before the first communion ceremony.

Luckily, I passed the initial screening test with our priest at the end of our 'Catéchis' classes. During my first confession, I told Fadda that I had engaged in sexual activities with three different men. My priest's jaw dropped, leading him to ask follow-up questions - *Who? What? When? Where? How? Did you bleed?* Naturally, I thought I had sinned because of what repeatedly happened to me, and I needed to confess those sins. There had to be something wrong with me, right? I must have been unclean. After Fadda accurately confirmed that I was not penetrated, he muttered a sigh of relief, and with an awkward smile, he reassured me that this was not true sex. He told me that I should never tell anyone about these experiences ever again. He then prayed for me.

As an adult, I shared in a blog post that I was not mad at my priest. I understood why he did it. He genuinely thought he was protecting me from the judgment of "church folks" if something so sensitive was leaked to the public. Often, when a group of people are attending a church, but their lives remain unchanged, a victim can become the scapegoat.

I walked down the aisle for my First Holy Communion Ceremony at my local Catholic church dressed in all white. I took pictures, smiled, had a great celebration party afterward, and continued living my life in silent shame.

Pour Me A Drink

Figure 4 - *Dancing while drunk at a local club in The Bahamas (2007)*

Alcohol was an engrained part of both my Haitian and Bahamian upbringing. We drank on special occasions, we drank when we were sad, we drank when we were happy, and we drank for the 'Homies' who died. In fact, my family began selling alcohol from our house before I was born. Interestingly enough, I started selling alcohol by the time I was four years old, and I picked up bottles of alcohol from suppliers for my mother by the time I was five. We carried an array of alcohol, including Kalik (esteemed beer of The Bahamas), Guinness, Heineken, and the punch to go along with it. Alcohol was simply a part of our lives.

I drank my first beer at the age of four from my father who offered it to me one day—it tasted gross. To this day, I still cannot understand how people appreciate the bitter taste of beer. Nonetheless, as I grew older, I started to enjoy an occasional swig of Kremas (a Haitian coconut cream-based drink usually offered at weddings and first communions).

To add insult to injury, my father was a very heavy drinker. My dad was known to be a strict man who barely smiled or showed emotion. Though he was home for my entire childhood, he felt distant emotionally and infrequently shared physical acts of love such as hugging or pats on the back. When he drank liquor though, he morphed into another being. While drunk, my father smiled from ear to ear, shared jokes, and shouted words of affirmation—you name it, my father displayed when he was drunk. The only issue with this is that he was also very boisterous and clumsy, leaving behind chaos and resentment when he was inebriated. My father drank often. There were many days when I wondered why my mother tolerated it. He never physically abused her, but on occasion, my siblings and I endured the brunt of his fists with lashes when he overdrank.

One night, my father drank so heavily that he dragged me on the floor by my left ankle and continuously beat me with his belt, which left me with a highly impressive black eye. My mother took me to the clinic the next day where I was cautioned to say that I hit my eye on the drawer running from my little brother. It was common for us to be left with bruises and scars from my father's drunken episodes.

Fast forward to my senior year of high school. I was a straight-A student, earning numerous awards and immersed in diverse extracurricular activities. As I mentioned before, these helped me to escape the shame of my childhood trauma and the drama going on at home. It was during this time, near my 16th birthday that I also started hanging out with four other girls, affectionately called 'The Beaulahs'. We wore matching ponytail hairstyles when going to the local bowling alley and held sleepovers at each other's houses. It felt amazing to have friends to teach me about womanhood, make-up, and boys. I finally started to feel as if I belonged, and our adventures were indescribable. While hanging out with this group of girls, I was introduced to a habit that would follow me into adulthood – drinking alcohol.

The legal drinking age in The Bahamas is eighteen, however, the laws were not always followed. I started drinking to fit in. Eventually, though, drinking became a way to numb my pain. Sadly, I learned to like the taste of alcohol. When I drank, I was free—from shame and drama. I drank almost any drink, except beer. I loved alcohol and alcohol loved me back. On weekends, the Beaulahs and I dressed up and went to the hottest nightclubs and house parties our island would allow. On the weekends, we drank until we could not drink any longer, danced until our knees buckled, met up with our favorite boys, and listened to Tanya Stephens, but we resumed our weekly scholastic activities as if nothing ever happened on Monday morning. The next weekend, we continued the cycle. Essentially, we were functioning alcoholics. After all, I was at the top of my class and made it look easy. It was only natural that I also gave drinking and partying my best shot with pure excellence.

My drinking became so severe that one night, after our usual partying as the Beaulahs were headed home, I became woozy. Suddenly the room started spinning around me. In an instant, I felt sick. I vomited in the backseat of my friend's sister's car. Embarrassed was the understatement of the century. To this day, the scent of the car's backseat has never recovered. I left my mark alright! On the night of my graduation from high school, I woke up after passing out in the back seat of one of the Beaulahs' car, right in front of her sister's apartment. We were so drunk we did not sleep in a bed that night. I do not remember how we got home, as we were all intoxicated. Can you say, astonishing? I recovered from my hangover that day only to discover that I was featured on the front page of our local newspaper for my high school valedictorian speech. Yes, I had many accolades and accomplishments, but I was broken and deeply confused, searching for validation and adventure in the most toxic ways.

Adolescence is usually a time for self-discovery, and it can be quite overwhelming, but there were better ways to channel my energy. I was developing self-deprecating habits and living for the approval of friends because I was running away from my emotional pain and trauma. Hanging out with the Beaulahs also introduced me to the greatest joys and deepest pains of my teenage life—my first love, Angel.

High school is definitely a delicate time. Adolescents begin exploring the notion of love and developing an infatuation for people of interest. The boys at my church showed interest and sometimes there was an occasional suitor at school, but I never really felt like I got the guy that I truly wanted. Since I was the tallest girl in my class, my typical type was tall, lanky with medium build, and preferably a basketball player. Unfortunately, they were not interested in the class nerd. In my mind, I fantasized about a marriage with the tallest boy in school. Despite my fantasy, these boys were rarely interested in a girl with a 4.0 GPA who was incredibly tall, and according to one of my classmates, "Nice, but ugly". To say this dampened my self-esteem was a gross understatement.

One day, a fellow Beaulah told me she had the perfect guy for me. She shared that he was tall, with smooth, dark-skinned, straight pearly white teeth and he was "dreamy." Of course, I was intrigued. So, my friend introduced me to this 'Hotty' named Angel. We began talking on the house phone weekly, but that turned into daily conversations lasting hours. I waited until my parents were asleep to sneak away to the telephone to chat with this guy (at the time we used house phones with a cord). We talked about everything, from our dreams and aspirations, our hobbies, past relationships, and how we wanted to raise a family. This went on for about a month, but I had never met him in person. I only saw him through Hi-5, the social media platform at that time, and he was indeed tall, dark, and dreamy.

One thing my friend left out was that he not only smoked marijuana, but sold it as well. Yes, my boyfriend was a drug dealer. After a month of talking, Angel suggested we meet up at our local fair (we called it a carnival) for our first date. I had never been on a date before, and I was rather enjoying our conversations, so I agreed to meet him. My Beaulahs helped me get ready for the big day. One of my Beaulahs' mothers styled my hair, another Bealuah did my make-up and another bought me an olive green shirt with a deep V-neck that showed a hint of cleavage.

Man, by the time I entered the carnival lot, I did not recognize myself! I was shocked to see that I was this beautiful. Up until that point, I never felt beautiful. Sadly, life always had a way of reminding me that I was worthless and that nobody really cared for me despite my achievements. That night, standing at the carnival waiting on my beau made me feel like the most beautiful girl in the world.

I waited. I walked around the carnival with my friends. Many of my classmates did not recognize me. I sent text messages to Angel to find out where he wanted to meet, and I waited. He never responded. My friends and I walked around the fair until my feet grew tired. I waited a little while longer, but Angel never showed up. Standing there in all my glory, in front of my Beaulahs being stood up by the first boy I was romantically interested in was one of the greatest letdowns of my life, up until that point.

So, we did what we usually did to solve our problems—we drank. My girls and I decided to hit up the nearest bar, where I took a few shots of my favorite drink, tequila. We left the bar and went to the local bowling alley. Guess who was there all dressed and 'posted up' with his boys? Angel! One of my Beaulahs pointed him out and I immediately bolted toward him.

I was already drunk at this point and boldly, I walked up to Angel demanding an explanation. How could he be so calm and comfortable and alive without responding to my text all while standing me up? This was the first time I had even met the boy in person and although I was embarrassed and furious, he was captivating. Angel looked even better in person. Standing in front of me was a 6'1" caramel-skinned, scrawny boy with thick black eyelashes and the straightest white teeth. His cologne was alluring, and his 'swag' was evident. Maybe it was the alcohol, perhaps it was my unaddressed shame, but whatever it was, I admired this beautiful mess standing in front of me. For the duration of our night out, I followed Angel and continued having casual conversations, as if nothing went wrong that night.

Fast forward to the following weekend when the alcohol wore off and I had more time to think about my embarrassment, Angel messaged me on MSN Messenger with a 'half-assed' apology. He shared that he could not find a ride and the only reason he made it to the bowling alley that night was because his friend was driving and forced him to go out. He did not want to be a burden to his friend by having him drop him off at the carnival. I could not believe that I was stood up on my first date. The embarrassment was too much. So, I broke up with my love on MSN Messenger because, I realized, at least for a moment that I loved myself more than I loved that relationship.

However, I missed him. Angel caught a glimpse of some photos I posted on the website, Hi-5 a few weeks later and he called me to talk. I shared one of my unwritten love letters with him, pouring out my heart about how he hurt me, and we agreed not to hurt each other again. We decided to try the relationship one more time. The second time was rockier than the first. It started well, as we resumed our deep conversations about the future and shared our deepest secrets. Angel and I met up on a few rendezvous, commonly called a 'Ghost move' in the Bahamas where we engaged in heavy petting. He knew I was a virgin and did not force me to go beyond my limits. Angel loved smoking weed. Each time we met up, consisted of him rolling up a joint, which left the taste of his weed on my breath.

I did not realize how deep into this lifestyle Angel was until he disappeared for a week. It went from us talking often and falling asleep at night with each other on the phone to him not returning my text messages or phone calls. I remember it like it was this morning. It was a rough week not hearing from my Boo. At the time, the song "Do you" by Neyo was playing non-stop in my bedroom as I cried over my long-lost love. On another occasion, I was so heartbroken from being 'ghosted' by my lover that I drank six tequila shots in a row with my Beaulahs. I was a total mess.

I later found out that Angel had been arrested and was in jail during this period. He was found with weed in his possession and had to spend a few days behind bars before getting bailed out. I was so deeply in love with this beautiful mess that I did not know whether to be happy he had a 'good' reason for being missing in action, or to cry for the reason he was behind bars. Isn't it amazing that the top student in her high school class was attracted to such a toxic relationship?

Unaddressed pain, immature company, and false self-identity, combined with plain stupidity will drive many adolescents and young adults to reckless behavior and toxic 'situationships' that can become permanent. Yes, I was living in dysfunction, even with my excellent performance in school and all my other accolades. What finally made me end the relationship with Angel was not his love for marijuana, the fact that he sold it, nor that I knew he had a "Side chick" he was having sex with. I figured, at least I was the "main chick", and I could claim him openly. Since he was not having sex with me, then he was allowed to get "it" elsewhere… right? I lost my love for myself and discarded my value over six months. There were rumors about Angel being in relationships with other girls, but I assumed it was his known "Side chick". I had convinced myself that this was something that every Bahamian man engaged in.

On the eve of his birthday, however, Angel confessed that I was not his main girlfriend. He and another girl were in a committed relationship for years before meeting me, but he told me he was willing to give her up to keep me because he did not want to lose me. I was already lost. I lost who I was and what my worth was. I lost me, looking to save him. I lost so much already to stay with him, and I did not have anything more to lose. I ended it with Angel that night. Since we never engaged in sexual intercourse, I surmised that my vow to God was still valid. Angel later died of complications from a car accident while driving drunk 10 years later.

The reality of my senior year of high school was setting in for me. I was a top student, with seven college acceptances, and no scholarships to my name. I did not receive any financial aid from the private high school I attended and the financial means to pay for my college education simply was not there. My parents felt the burden of my gift. They realized that our "hustle" was not enough to cover tuition costs. At age 16, I was ambitious and talented, but this was not enough for me to further my dream of becoming a medical doctor. I needed money.

II. Lessons

♦ We have a real enemy who seeks to steal, kill, and destroy us, especially at a young age, and I believe wholeheartedly that this enemy is Satan. He is the spirit behind childhood trauma (sexual, emotional, physical abuse, etc.) that seeks to silence, stagnate, and suffocate young children well into their adulthood.

♦ Never be ashamed of what happened to you as a child. It is not your fault. Your voice matters. You have value. You are worthy. You are enough.

♦ Adults, if children share traumatic experiences with you, please validate their pain, and believe them. Please share this information with the proper authorities who can intervene on that child's behalf. Likewise, seek the professional help of a licensed counselor to help this child process his/her feelings rather than burying them. See Appendix for further resources for survivors of child sexual abuse and those who may be raising them.

♦ Trauma needs to be processed (grieved, talked through, validated, supported, given healthy coping mechanisms), not buried.

♦ It is NOT your fault what happened to you as a child, but it IS your responsibility to heal from childhood trauma.

♦ Avoid friends who enable you to participate in self-destructive habits, as you will become the company you keep.

♦ Avoid alcohol and substance abuse. Their effects on your mind and body are simply not worth it in the end. It is okay to say "No", even if you feel left out as this "No" could save your life.

♦ You do not have to do everything your friends do to fit in. Mentorship matters. Seek wise counsel from older teachers, coaches, and faith leaders to help you navigate life's journey.

♦ Keep seeking God in high school through prayer and reading the Bible for yourself.

- Talk to a trusted adult about the hormones and feelings that you are having for the opposite sex and ask them to help you navigate these emotions, rather than getting this information from friends or the media.

- Parents, communicate with your children about hormones, attractions, and sexual relationships. If you are uncomfortable having these conversations then arrange for your child to have these discussions with wise, wholesome counselors or leaders. Otherwise, they will learn from friends, social media, culture, and magazines, which can be very destructive.

- Your kids are learning about sex either way, so be intentional about leading their influences.

Chapter III

Miracles -
First Generation
College Students

Figure 5 - *Ebony and Gina posing in front of*
our college sign during freshman year (2007).
Who knew we would be best friends ever since!

I f I did not already mention, I was born in Miami, Florida, but raised in The Bahamas. My mother was on vacation in Florida when her water broke, and she delivered me at Jackson Memorial Hospital in Miami. Because of this, I always had an American passport, and as such, I was not a formal citizen of The Bahamas, which is why, when I graduated from high school as the valedictorian, I did not receive many scholarship opportunities to attend college from the Bahamas. This was highly disheartening, considering how hard I worked, my many awards, and the fact that I had been accepted to seven colleges in South Florida. I graduated high school in June 2007 and had no idea where I was going next, or how I was going to get there. My parents were regretful because they knew how gifted I was and yet, they did not have the money to send me to school. Also, I was depressed because I had recently ended it with my first love, Angel, and I strongly desired to pursue my education. Unfortunately, the money was just not there. I was disoriented, hurt, ashamed, and moody the whole summer. At the time, I was considering finding a summer job while I figured out my next step and I still maintained some relationships with my teachers from high school. One day, as I was venting to my English teacher, Mrs. Evans, about my dilemma, she randomly shared that she knew a wealthy family who had a scholarship foundation in The Bahamas and encouraged me to write a letter to them concerning my predicament. Mrs. Evans knew how hard I worked and could not bear to see me in such pain. She reviewed my letter and sent it to the couple, who then set up a meeting with me via telephone and eventually in person. The couple agreed to add to whatever cost was missing from my college education after FAFSA (Free Application for Federal Student Aid) and funded my first year of college. They paid the balance of $10,000, which covered my room and board for the first year, but I had to figure out how to pay the remainder of my education thereafter. I was not concerned about that stipulation. Miraculously, I was on my way to college and God had made a way out of no way!

Our Gwoup Jen leader at the time, Ms. Lorena, threw a small going away party for me at her home in Freeport, shortly before I left. During this time, I also prayed for an amazing college roommate whom I would get along with, and for her to be a blessing to my life.

College

Navigating college was challenging and exhilarating. I was the first person in my family to attend post-secondary school. Additionally, I had never been this far away from my parents. Although I was a 45-minute flight or a 4-hour boat ride away from my parents, it still felt like we were two universes apart. College in South Florida represented the accomplishment of my childhood dreams, but it also exposed the wounds I buried. I beamed with pride the day I started Barry University, a private Catholic institution in Miami Shores, FL. There was no greater feeling imaginable. I was on cloud nine and this experience was so surreal.

On the first day of college, as I was opening the door to my room, a short, light-skinned girl wearing a satin wrap tied over her head walked in. "Oh, you live here?" she asked, in the thickest Southern accent I had ever heard. I replied, "Yes. OMG, are you my roommate?" I gave her the biggest hug. If looks could kill, I would be dead. She barely hugged me back and she gave me a strange look as we both entered the room. Here we go, I thought.

I later found out that my new roommate's name was Ebony Harris. She was from Laurel Maryland. I was discouraged by how Ebony looked at me with distrust, but eventually, I learned that she just needed to warm up to new people. Ebony turned out to be the guardian angel I prayed for. We hung out often—at the cafeteria, the gym, at school parties, and we even ate Haitian food together. She was the answer to my prayer and remained my roommate for all 4 years of undergrad. Ebony was, and still is my best friend and confidante to this day. We frequently stayed up in our dorm room freshman year until 3 a.m., sometimes discussing our dreams of becoming a medical doctor, and an attorney. We often shared that one day we wanted to build the legacy for our own families that we wished we had growing up. To say that Ebony had my back in college and beyond does not do that statement justice. I gained a lifelong sister, and I am always grateful to God for that connection.

In my first year of undergrad, God continued to provide the grace for me to excel in my classes. I maintained a 4.0 GPA throughout my first two years of undergrad through sheer hard work and focus. Typically, I would sit in a quiet space in the library after class, where I studied and reviewed the material from my lessons until I had the key details memorized.

While in college, I also started having migraines—inherited from my father. There were periods of 1-3 months where I experienced sharp, stabbing pains on the left side of my head, which lasted for four hours. The only thing I could do was sleep it off. These migraines stopped me in my tracks, often causing me to rush to my dorm room, shut off the lights, and lay down in stillness until the headache subsided. Studying was sometimes debilitating, but thankfully, two Excedrin tablets helped to decrease the length of time the migraines lasted.

I continued to practice Catholicism in college and attended weekly masses for spiritual grounding. Sadly, although I was a frequent church attendee and an excellent student, I continued to be an avid drinker—tequila, vodka, shots, and mixed drinks remained my close companions. My suitemates and I often indulged in house parties on campus and sometimes had drink-offs in our dorm rooms.

Of course, college consisted of the usual: classes, lunch at the cafeteria, collegiate sports, parties, and boys. One day, as I was headed to the Student Union to work out during my freshman year, I lost my breath when I saw a 6'8" dark-skinned 'gift' from St. Kitts walking toward me from the basketball court named Jakari. At that moment, I knew he would be my husband (in my mind). I was obsessed with Jakari—his skin, his height, his 'swag', his accent, etc. "Who created this man?" I asked my suitemates. I could not get him out of my mind, and I took every opportunity to get to know him, but I could never seem to get any one-on-one time with Jakari. He was either at practice or with his boys. Furthermore, I had too much Caribbean pride to walk up to a boy and start a conversation. Culturally, I was so accustomed to boys making the first move in The Bahamas.

However, I soon found the courage that only alcohol could provide. One night, after one of our regular drinking sessions in our dorm, we were invited to Jakari's room by one of our suitemates who happened to be friends with Jakari's roommate. I put on the tightest pair of jeans and the 'flyest' blouse I could find, eager to seize on the opportunity to meet him. Likewise, one of my suitemates wore her shortest 'booty' shorts to the party. A group of us walked over to Jakari's room, where we hung out, kicked back, laughed, drank, and danced the night away. At the end of the night, somehow, the person who was too shy to talk to a boy first happened to be alone in Jakari's room with him. As his hands moved up and down my body, I politely told him I was a virgin and that I was not interested in having sex with him that night. He kindly stated, "You can suck it, then". Even with alcohol in my system, this request seemed so outlandish. I thought, who does this boy think I am?

What I truly should have considered was who I was NOT. I was not as sophisticated and self-confident as I had portrayed. I was not giving off 'Virtuous woman' vibes, even though I was attending church. I was meddling in areas where I had no business, and I kept opening myself up to too many racy situations. No! I did not suck 'it' that night or ever, for that matter. I walked out of the room unscathed, with my head held high. However, my suitemate who wore the booty shorts that night started dating and sleeping with Jakari the next week.

Needless to say, I repeatedly participated in racy activities with young men who should not have made it past "Hello". Heavy petting and near misses became my norm. I know now that these were all manifestations of unaddressed pain. I was numbing childhood trauma by drinking, partying, near-sexual mishaps. Jesus was calling me to him, but my resentment of what happened to me as a child did not give him room to touch this area of my life. It would be years until I faced these nasty habits. My drinking had become so intense, I remember attending mass intoxicated one day during my freshman year. Sadly, I was scheduled to do the 'First reading' of the word at the altar that night. When I got up to read the scripture that night, I felt a burning sensation, like fire throughout my entire body. My hair, my skin, my chest, my stomach, and my feet were burning profusely. I could barely get the words out. This was one of the first signs I realized that hell was real, and that Jesus was trying to get my full attention. Hell was what I was living internally while portraying heaven externally.

To add fuel to fire, that was also the year when I experienced cruelty from one of my sponsors. When I first started college, my sponsors gave me a cell phone to contact my family in case of an emergency. Clearly, I was a social butterfly, and often used the phone to text my friends. My sponsor scolded me for using my phone so frequently and threatened to take it back if I continued to overuse it. When I did not comply, all hell broke loose! My sponsor talked negatively about me to Mrs. Evans, my English teacher who helped me get the scholarship. However, the most hurtful experience came toward the end of my freshman year.

As my roommate and I were cleaning out our dorm room, my sponsor agreed to hold a few items in their shed for the summer. After packing my personal items in boxes and bins, my roommate and I carried them downstairs to put them in my sponsor's car. My sponsor, who was a middle-aged white woman, asked my roommate to leave because she had to speak with me privately. While we were alone, she unleashed on me. "Look at how filthy these boxes were packed. It's as if an animal did this. I need you to step it up Gina," she said with her palms lifted to the sky. "There are plenty of other gifted and smart kids out here who can pack better than you, who are more appreciative than you, and who are more respectful than you. It's not enough to tell us that you are a 4.0 student. We need to see proof, so please give us a copy of your transcripts. I mean, you just need to step it up, Gina. We are paying for your education here. I mean, this is more than your father will ever make in a year." I smiled at her comments, and she scolded me again for smiling, saying, "Your smiling is coming across as being disrespectful."

After this conversation with my sponsor, I walked straight to my dorm room, locked myself in the bathroom, and cried. It broke me to hear someone who appeared to be so caring, belittle me for the generous acts she and her husband were so pleased to perform at first. Should I have clapped back? Should I have fought with her? Should I have dropped out of school? This was one of my first encounters with a white woman in America who carried an air of control and 'ownership' over me, which, by default, felt suppressive. This experience definitely felt racially tense, but truthfully, I needed her. My sponsors were paying for an education my family could not afford. So, I 'licked my wounds and kept it moving.' I continued to excel academically and eventually got a new cell phone on my own, without the hassle of being monitored like the oppressed.

Thankfully, I graduated from Barry University, debt-free because this couple paid the remaining balance of my undergraduate education each year. Truly college was not all dysfunctional. Despite the challenges I faced personally, I still achieved numerous accolades. For instance, I was the president of our Haitian Student Organization at Barry University known as the Haitian Inter-Cultural Association

(HICA) for two years, alongside a fellow group of bright leaders. We met weekly with 10 - 20 students to plan events and perform community service activities. In 2010, we won the Best Event of The Year award for raising money for families impacted by the terrible earthquake that killed hundreds of thousands of people in Haiti on January 12th, 2010. I won the President of the Year award at that same time.

My extra-curricular life further blossomed as I was involved in research as part of a minority research program called Research Initiative for Scientific Enhancement (RISE) that allowed me to apply and travel nationally to participate in summer research programs and national conferences. I even performed research on campus with Professor Leticia Vega who was an incredible Principal Investigator. In the RISE program, I attended two summer internships at Vanderbilt University in Nashville Tennessee, and an internship at the prestigious Johns Hopkins University in Baltimore, MD. One year at Vanderbilt, I won the Poster of The Year award for my ongoing research with telomeres in yeast, studying their longevity and link to cancer. And, of course, my grades continued to flourish. By God's grace, I graduated Barry University with a Summa Cum Laude distinction, wrapping up my college years with a 3.91 GPA.

In addition, due to my academic achievements and dedicated community service, I was awarded the St. Catherine Medal for leadership at Barry University, along with the Dean's Award and the Most Outstanding Biology Major Award. Your girl was smart! I cannot list all of the awards I won as it would take up many chapters of this book—too many. As He did before, God continued to grace me throughout my college years, despite my humble beginnings and questionable personal life.

III. Lessons

- God provides. Keep praying and seeking his will for your life. No matter the situation you are facing, God will provide.

- Get familiar with and read the Bible for yourself rather than depending on others to teach you. Have your own personal and intimate relationship with Jesus Christ.

- Unaddressed childhood trauma and shame will show up in your life and is a sign that healing needs to take place. Whether you choose to address this default setting is up to you.

- Don't judge those around you who appear to make negative life choices in the form of promiscuity, substance abuse, or mental anguish. You simply never know what that person is or has experienced.

- Pray for those who seem to be acting out of character. Jesus cares deeply and is near the hurting, lost, and brokenhearted.

- Teachers who take a compassionate interest in the lives of their students are worthy of praise, honor, and respect. My English Teacher Mrs. Evans and elementary school Teaher Mrs. Moxey are proof of the major difference teachers can make in the lives of their students.

♦ Parents, as much as possible, please save up for your children's future. Even a little goes a long way.

♦ Find a good mentor in college to help you navigate your major, career goals, and life after graduation.

♦ Joining interest groups in college can expand your network of friends and social skills.

♦ Substance use, and destructive sexual practices in college are not worth it. It's better to channel your time and energy into more productive habits.

Chapter IV

Rejected

Figure 6 *- Gina at the Honors and Convocation Ceremony Senior year of college (May 2011)*

Since Freeport was merely a 45-minute flight from Miami, I went home to visit The Bahamas often. During one of these visits, I reconnected with a childhood friend, Neo, whose father was super close to my family. Neo had caramel skin, and he was a smooth talker. He was shorter than me and acknowledged that I was a tall girl. Although Neo was always interested in me, we never seemed to hit it off. My encounters with him mainly consisted of long stares, smiles, and small talk. However, on this particular trip, Neo kept coming over to our house. At one point, he expressed his unwavering love for me and shared that he was ready to be in a relationship with me.

I had a favorite spot on the bay in my neighborhood where our town gathered every Thursday night for a 'Fish Fry'. This is where I often went to meditate. It was a rocky area, but a true Bahamian gem surrounded by blue-green water that was as peaceful as can be. It was at this spot on the bay that I went to often to think about Neo's request. I decided that it probably was not a bad idea to give him a chance, given how close we grew up. He definitely knew how amazing I was, right? 'Chal', I ignored the fact that Neo was trying to establish a relationship with me while he was already in committed relationships with other girls. At the time I was considering dating him, he was not in a relationship. Obviously, unaddressed trauma played a significant role in this connection.

One night after my childhood friend, Edna had finished doing my hair, I prayed a simple prayer: *Lord, if Neo is the man you have for me to marry, please show me.* I then proceeded to walk over to Neo's house in Eight Mile Rock where we were casually talking and 'catching the breeze'. Suddenly, I heard a loud knock at Neo's door along with a female's voice. Neo did not respond. Shortly after, a little girl jumped through a window in his house and opened the door. In walked a short, stubby, and loud young lady I had never seen before. The young lady attempted to fight me, but Neo blocked her with his body. She grew louder and louder screaming, "Neo, wasn't it just last week we were messing around?" She started pushing Neo as she cried. I immediately texted my big brother to pick me up. Clearly, this was the sign I needed, but Neo drove to my home that night to talk. He explained that we had not agreed to a committed relationship yet when he was with the young woman, so I should not hold it against him. I told him that I would think long and hard about being with him but being the 'bright' young lady I was, I became Neo's girlfriend before I left Freeport that winter.

This was a poor decision on my part. For another six months, I was involved in a very rocky and unnecessary relationship with someone who should have remained an associate. However, this relationship was a defining moment for me because it was the deepest level of intimacy I had experienced with a man at this point. Neo and I eventually engaged in oral sex one night and as he was stimulating parts of my body that I did not know existed, I was introduced to masturbation. Neo never penetrated me, but we did come extremely close one night.

As I recalled the promise I made to God at the age of fourteen (to watch over my grades and I would remain a virgin until marriage), my stomach turned at how far I had drifted away with my life's choices. Ultimately Neo got another girl pregnant (a different one from the one who tried to fight me). He told me about the pregnancy via a text message he sent to me the weekend after he and I were intimate. That was all I needed to walk away from this toxic situation. God warns us and he tries to protect us with his "No". His words, His teachings in the Bible to refrain from fornication, and His waving of red flags are for our divine protection. Listen to God's warnings.

Moving forward, the summer of 2010 was when I completed another summer internship, this time at Johns Hopkins University. During this experience, I studied and sat for the Medical College Admission Test (MCAT), which is a standardized test needed in the United States to gain admission to medical school. I attended a biology lab as a part of my research internship during the day and studied for the MCAT in the evening and on the weekends. While my friends were hanging out and getting to know one another in the evenings after work, I was home flipping through Kaplan and Exam Crackers, attempting to prepare for this exam.

Usually, applicants to medical school take the MCAT the year before the anticipated start date and submit this score along with their medical school application to allow enough time for interviews and eventual admission to medical school. I took my MCAT the summer after my junior year of college, July 2010 but I did not do well. My score was marginal, but I assumed I would be okay, given my high academic performance and a plethora of extracurricular activities.

I did not have mentors when I was applying to medical school and so, I was truly 'winging it' with my application. Furthermore, I applied to mainly top-tier schools and barely had a medical professional review my Personal Statement before submitting my application. I fell into the trap of becoming overconfident with my performance and assumed that the application process would work out for me, just as it did so many times before. After all, I was accepted to all seven colleges I applied to for my undergrad degree, and I performed so stellar throughout high school and college. Who wouldn't want me?

With the countless awards, achievements, and accolades I accrued at Barry University and in high school, I was unanimously rejected from all fourteen medical schools I applied to. Yes, I was graduating Suma Cum Laude from a stellar college, and at the same time being rejected from the only profession I was studying so hard to get into. Quiet as it's kept, I was also still recovering from the shame of not choosing a quality life partner to marry by the time I graduated college. It was during my senior year of college when I hit rock bottom. I faced constant questions from my research advisors, wanting to know if I heard from any medical schools. I was also asked if

I had considered other professions since I had not gotten any positive responses from the medical schools I applied to. Even my family was curious about the next steps of my life, and I honestly had no response. I was so used to having all the answers in my life and moving in a forward trajectory that this place of rejection and the unknown was difficult. Naturally, I turned to my usual escape mechanisms, alcohol and 'Situation-ships'.

Master's Degree –
"Grown-ish"

Luckily, when I was finishing up college, one of my advisors suggested that I apply to post-baccalaureate programs, (otherwise know as, a post-bacc) as a back-up plan. As a result, I was accepted into Drexel University's Medical Science Program (MSP). A post-baccalaureate program is a 1 or 2-year program where students who desire to go to medical school or some other doctoral program could enroll to improve their application if their college GPA or MCAT scores were not competitive.

Immediately after graduating from Barry University, however, I spent the summer at home in Eight Mile Rock. While there, I had two more 'flings' with a crush from elementary school and another crush who used to play basketball at another private high school back in the day. Shamelessly, I was out almost every weekend that summer, drinking to my heart's content. Shortly in late July, I kissed my summer flings goodbye and flew to Philadelphia to start the MSP program at Drexel University.

The first year in Philly was rough. Thanks to my generous sponsors, up to this point, I was debt-free. During this post-bacc was the first time I applied for student loans to pay for my tuition and any refund I received was to be used for room and board. I was broke. The Dollar Tree became my favorite store. Many nights I ate bread and butter or baked beans for dinner because it was all I could afford. I also did not have money for furniture, so I slept on an air mattress with a box spring that was donated by someone who was moving out of their apartment. Craig's List was also another favorite discount option for quick, cheap furniture. The sacrifices were endless as I pursued my dream of becoming a medical doctor so far away from home.

Somehow, I and the group of friends I made at Drexel found enough cash for drinks and partying. While I excelled in my higher-level graduate classes and built rapport with great professors, I also enjoyed the scene and great food of Old Town Philly and continued to 'turn up' on weekends. My outfits grew particularly skimpy, short, and tight. Nevertheless, I continued to attend mass every Sunday morning at a local Catholic church, as I perpetually found myself living a double life. I was 'doing the most' at all the parties -'dropping it low' on the dance floor every weekend. Of course, I had a crush or two during my post-bacc, but for some reason, these guys never seemed interested in me. It was likely due to my reputation as the party girl, but more often than not, their preference was typically for Asian, white, or mixed-race women. That's a story for another time.

My time in Philly was exhilarating and I had gained the reputation of being the life of the party with my group of friends. My clique was 'poppin'!'

One thing I appreciated about the master's program was the diversity of friends and the connections I made. South Florida and Barry University were also a great place to network, but by default, I mingled mostly with Haitians and Caribbean people. In Philly, I had a white friend from North Carolina, a suburbian Black friend from Ghana, a respectable Black 'Morehouse Man' from Detroit, a beloved sweet guy from Pakistan, and a gorgeous twin from Puerto Rico. Together we binged-watched TV shows, played board games, threw house parties, partied, got drunk, and, of course, studied. I was exposed to so many different cultures, which I appreciated after coming from the hood of Eight Mile Rock, Grand Bahama.

During my post-bacc, I took a Princeton Review Course to help me with my MCAT. The grind of studying was epic! This review course was taught by Mark, a graduate-level student who scored in the upper 99th percentile on the test. Mark was a white guy who was blunt and quite 'full of himself'. Dressed in his finest preppy sweaters and pressed khakis, Mark often reminded us that what came easy for him took others much more time to 'catch up.' He exuded sarcasm, enunciating each letter of his words with a dry sense of humor and a smirk. He believed he was the smartest person in the room at all times, and it showed. We completed chapters of the Princeton review book and reviewed test-taking strategies, such as crossing out answers we knew were incorrect, highlighting key phrases of the question being asked, and narrowing down our answer options based on contrasting statements. Mark also emphasized the importance of taking practice tests often, which I did not do the first time I studied for the MCAT. In a nutshell, it was imperative to time yourself while taking a test as it was knowing the various topic matters.

I appreciated this Princeton review course because it highlighted my standardized test-taking weaknesses and helped me to fill in the gaps as we went along.

Thankfully, I sat for the MCAT in the Spring of 2012 and scored 4 points higher, enough for me to apply and eventually get interview offers from two schools. Since 2012, the MCAT has changed from a 2-digit to a 3-digit scoring system. (See Appendix for pre-med tips and updated scoring info.)

As I mentioned in the previous chapter, it takes one year before your start date to apply to medical school, factoring time needed for secondary applications and potential interviews. Secondary applications comprise of a set of specific questions individual medical schools ask you to submit prior to offering you an interview. The post-bacc program at Drexel was a year-long program and once completed, many people either worked or extended their educational journey by a second year, enrolling in a master's curriculum while waiting to be interviewed for medical school. In my case, it did not work out with the research jobs I was applying for, and I did not want to go back to Freeport where distractions awaited me. So, at the very last minute, I applied for a master's program in Health Sciences at Drexel University, opting to stay for a second year. Choosing to do a master's program stacked on another round of student loans for me, which was another sacrifice in pursuing my dream of becoming a medical doctor. Indeed, the accruing of more student loan debt is stressful and can deter many from pursuing the field of medicine, but I calculated the cost, and this was the best course of action for me to build up my foundation and connections for the next part of my journey. In due time, I figured I would earn enough to pay off my student loan debt.

Isolation

My most memorable experience during my master's program was encountering Christ, for real. Because I decided to apply for the master's program at the last minute, my student loan refund disbursement was also delayed. Like many students, I relied on these funds for my cost of living (i.e. food, rent, books, etc.). I was a broke college student, and unfortunately, my lease in the dorm room I stayed in prior was up.

I began my master's program that summer with a 3.91 GPA, no money, homeless, and a deeply emptied soul. Thankfully, my gorgeous Puerto Rican friend, who was a twin, Katrina, allowed me to stay at her apartment until I received my first reimbursement check and was able to pay for my own apartment. I slept on Katrina's living room couch for about six weeks. Thankfully, I continued going to class and my grades excelled. I signed up for a Teacher's Assistant position and tutoring jobs, which helped me earn extra cash. My love for subjects like anatomy, cell biology, and histology soared and I consumed the material like my life depended on it.

In my free time, I surfed the internet and watched YouTube videos. One night, I came across a woman named Heather Lindsey. She was a light-skinned lady with hazel eyes who looked like a model. Heather was known for waiting until marriage to kiss her very attractive husband. I thought this was a hoax, given how attractive they both were. Yet, I was intrigued. She shared how she overcame her struggles with promiscuity and had a season of isolation with God to know him for herself. One video led to the next and before I knew it my soul began to feel alive again. After being numbed for so long with alcohol and risky behaviors, I felt the pulling of the Lord in my Spirit, right there on Katrina's couch, which led me to dig deeper and get closer to him like never before.

As the weeks went on, I eventually found a beautiful 4-bedroom townhouse ten minutes away from Drexel's campus. A fellow student was living there and shared with Katrina that she and her roommates were looking for another tenant. The townhouse had four stories, a rooftop, open windows, a spacious kitchen, massive bathroom spaces, more importantly, it was peaceful. Two male students, along with my female classmate lived there. We each occupied a separate floor of the home. Katrina helped me move in after we picked up furniture we found on Craig's list with our rented U-Haul. This was my first time living in an apartment off campus. Before this, I had always lived in a dorm room within a short walking distance of my classes. Being off campus felt like I had matured, and with my newfound interest in Heather Lindsey's teachings, something new began to happen in my life.

There, in the confines of the suite in my new apartment, I decided to get to know God personally. I gathered flashcards, a huge 200-sheet binder, highlighters, and pens I purchased from Office Depot and began the process of journaling, reading my Bible, and praying. I got up before class to read the Bible for myself, rather than depend on pre-written devotionals like the Daily Bread I grew up with. In my quest to know Jesus more intimately, I started reading the book of John. I wrote scriptures that stood out to me on one side of an index card and how I thought it applied to me on the back. At night, I wrote about my day in my journal and told God about the desires of my heart. I also prayed about my concerns about getting into medical school, having solid friendships, and being free from unhealthy coping mechanisms, such as alcoholism and masturbation, which I picked up reflexively to soothe my hurt. Because I was no longer living on campus, I lost connection with some of the friends I went partying with just a few months prior.

God met me in that beautiful townhouse on Melon Street in Philadelphia. My circle of friends changed, and I started attending a non-denominational Christian church in a basement with a preacher who spoke about prophecy, being world changers, and holding on to God's word. This was completely different from the classic mass, hymns, pre-selected scripture readings, and the focus on Mother Mary that I grew up with in the Catholic church. For the first time in my life, I felt so much peace. I was now living a lifestyle and exhibiting patterns that focused on a closer relationship with Jesus. I now felt like I could approach Jesus as a friend. While reading the book of John, I saw his humanity, confidence, sacrifice, and leadership in a whole new way. Additionally, I felt like Jesus saw me— my flaws, insecurities, personality traits, and my heart were all on display before him. Bare. Throughout my master's program, I slowly gave up partying on the weekends, quit drinking, stopped dressing so provocatively, and started fellowshipping with like-minded Christian women.

Soon enough, those around me noticed the shift. In fact, I went to dinner with my previous group of friends one night and they were shocked to see that I was not drinking. "Are you afraid Jesus will get mad at you?" asked one of my friends. I smiled and responded, "I'm just trying something new." My friends were headed out to the club after dinner but when I said I would be going home instead, everyone's faces froze. What I read on their faces was, *'Who is this new person, and where is our party girl?'*

Having an intimate relationship with Jesus will transform you, not only in your own eyes but also in the eyes of those around you. My friends and family could visibly see the evidence of my new life and I slowly began to lose the appetite for behaviors that once gave me so much pleasure. I finally saw how my old way of living was, in all actuality, destructive to my future. In this place of solace, Jesus began to sanctify me. It was difficult, at times, because I did not have much of a social life as I once did and sometimes, I missed having friends to call on and go out with on the weekends. Yet, in reading the Bible I understood that I was never fully alone. God is always near, and it was up to me to acknowledge his presence through prayer, fasting, and meditating on His word. These habits did not come naturally to me. Due to my upbringing in the more ritualistic practices of Catholicism, I was unfamiliar with this intimate rhythm of communing with God. Some days were easier than others, but overall, I did not feel as empty and thirsty on the inside as I did just months before.

During this season, I turned down two potential dating prospects who were tall, dark, and handsome, which was unheard of for me. I would have gladly entertained these men before. However, in that period of my life, I decided to get to know Jesus more intimately before rummaging through the lives of others to appease my brokenness.

My newfound love for Jesus and changing lifestyle also trickled its way into my classes. I vividly remember taking a leadership development course taught by one of the most confident and powerful women I have ever met. My professor, Dr. Sarita Lyons, gave us assignments on leadership skills, paired us into groups to achieve tasks as a team, and challenged us to question our normal tendencies while being okay with practicing new habits.

I remember a time when each of us had to give a presentation on a specific leader of our choice. For this particular assignment, I presented, "The Leadership

Qualities of Esther: Women in Leadership in The Bible". In this presentation, I broke down the loyal, compassionate, empathetic, courageous, and strategic leadership qualities of Esther. My classmates not only heard about the specific leadership style of Esther, but they also learned about a story in the Bible. In this instance, my peers got a bird's eye view of my transformation, and they also experienced the fruits of my personal time with God. I felt like I had found my identity.

Last, but certainly not least, I started to get interview offers to medical school for the first time during my master's program. This time, I applied to a broader and more strategic list of schools and my MCAT score increased by 4 points, which was slightly better (though not the greatest). Two out of twenty schools offered me an interview—Howard University in D.C. and Florida International University in Miami, Florida. I first interviewed at Howard University in the Fall of 2012. I was still broke, beaming, but brave. The week of my interview, I traveled from Philadelphia to D.C. on the Megabus, which cost about $10 one-way. I spent the night with my best friend's mother in Maryland. I purchased a suit on clearance from

Burlington Coat Factory the night before and took the train to D.C. the morning of the interview.

Based on the schedule that was sent to me, I prepared as best as I could the week before by reviewing the school's website, researching the instructors who were interviewing me, jotting down key elements that stood out and preparing a list of questions to ask during the day. Howard University was nothing short of a dream come true. On interview day, we toured the campus with our tour guide, ate in the hospital cafeteria on 'Wing Wednesday', and for the first time, met with Black doctors who looked like me. Until this point, all the doctors I had encountered were White or Indian. I was also ecstatic to see a diverse group of medical students who interviewed alongside me that day. There was one interviewee who stood out to me. As you might expect, he was tall, handsome, so very down to earth, and happened to be a Bahamian.

Things were looking up. I left Howard University on cloud nine at the possibility that this would be my new school. I reflected on my upbringing in Eight Mile Rock and the trauma that attached itself to me during childhood. I thought about the miracle of graduating college as a first-generation college student and certainly how far I had come in my spirit. God had truly been faithful.

Two short months later, by God's grace, I received my acceptance letter to Howard University Medical School. Once again, during my period of isolation, God showed up and showed out for me like never before. It turned out to be a transformational blessing. I was one step closer to becoming Dr. Guillaume. God found His way through my brokenness, false identity, rejections, and even my accomplishments to lift my spirit and He truly gave me 'beauty for my ashes'. If you are thinking about quitting, don't. With God, all things are truly possible.

IV. Lessons

♦ Rejection is God's redirection for your life. He uses this for a greater purpose. Even God's 'No' is for your protection and advancement. Eventually your feelings will catch up to God's promises.

♦ When facing rejection and disappointment, take a deep look at your character and your intentions for pursuing this dream. Are they pure? Why or why not?

♦ Do not give up on yourself or your dream.

♦ Keep seeking the Lord and getting to know him personally.

♦ Avoid making impulsive decisions and going back to familiar self-destructive habits when feeling isolated.

♦ Surround yourself with positive, productive, and purposeful people during times of isolation.

♦ Sometimes isolation provides fuel for your dreams and strengthens your character if you stay on the course.

- ◆ Rejection is a normal process. It happens to everybody. Stop beating yourself up for something that happens to many.
- ◆ Use rejection as an opportunity for growth rather than tearing yourself down or aborting your dreams.
- ◆ Everything has a purpose, including rejection.
- ◆ Learn test-taking strategies as early as possible, not just the information.

Chapter V

Mecca

Figure 7- Gina in her Short White Coat at Howard University College of Medicine (2015)

I graduated from Drexel with a 3.95 GPA in a new space of hope, a love for Jesus, and my eyes on the prize—medical school. Unquestionably, I was on cloud nine at the thought that I was accepted to THE Howard University, which was the best gift of my life thus far. At Howard University, all hues of Black excellence flooded the hallways, classrooms, and hospitals. Howard was such a significant place because it was founded at a time when our forefathers who attended this Historically Black College & University (HBCU) were not allowed to go to the same schools as their white counterparts. From the entrance, I was greeted with photos of these forefathers on the walls.

Pictures of greats like of Dr. Charles Drew, who excelled in the field of blood transfusions and storage adorned our lecture halls and hallways. Another great, the late Dr. Lori Wilson, the first woman to be promoted to full professor in surgery at Howard University Hospital, who taught us during our surgical rotations was a gift. Dr. Wilson later died of metastatic breast cancer in 2022—the very same illness she helped heal many women from in her surgical practice. I also had the privilege and blessing to attend lectures taught by the late Dr. LaSalle D. Leffall Jr., who was the first

Black American to serve as national President of the American Cancer Society (ACS). Dr. Leffall's famous phrase "Equanimity under duress" is still one of my key mantras to date. Without question, there was a spirit of Black excellence, pride, and belonging at Howard University that envelops you while you are there. Even our Financial Aid Advisor, a beautiful and stylish woman from Grenada met each student with a gracious smile.

There was no place better to be than at Howard University College of Medicine. Many of us were first-generation doctors, which made the moment even more special. Our friends and family gathered to attend our Short White Coat (induction) Ceremony before the start of the freshman semester year of medical school. My Haitian mother who flew in from Eight Mile Rock, Bahamas beamed with pride the entire day, considering our roots of poverty, tenacity, and hope. That day, a young woman raised in one of the poorest town in The Bahamas stood as a first-year medical student, along with her mother, an immigrant from the poorest country in the Western Hemisphere. God was truly with us.

Yet, the greatest love and gift I received from Howard University College of Medicine were my peers.

Our recruiter for the class of 2017 did well. In my medical school classes, I encountered some of the brightest, God-fearing, down-to-earth, 'ratchet', and unanimously excellent people. From the start of medical school, I was blessed to have a roommate, Tiffany, whose dream was to be a dermatologist. Her smile could light up a galaxy. When I was waiting for my refund check during the first few weeks of school, my beautiful roommate allowed me to sleep on her futon until my funds were available. It was evident from the start that we had each other's back. Thankfully, I never experienced the cut-throat practices that many of my counterparts experienced at predominantly white institutions.

Another gem that came from my time in Washington, D.C. was a great appreciation of African culture. I attended a Nigerian church called, Jesus House DC, which exposed me to all types of 'gele' (head wraps), Ankara (African printed clothing), and my favorite, jollof rice. Many of my classmates were of Nigerian and Ghanian descent and consistently played Afrobeats, which is West African music with the perfect blend of jazz and funk. Afrobeats is easily one of my favorite genres of music to date. Of course, I also had classmates who were Haitian. We hosted annual Haitian potlucks and get togethers in between our study breaks. Some of my closest friends though, included Linelle, a 'Mango-skinned' gyal from Trinidad, and Felicia, my beautiful Black American 'fashionista' from Philly.

I hung out with Felicia often. In fact, because she wore her hair in dreadlocks during medical school, I was encouraged to stop adding chemicals to my hair and embrace my "natural" hair texture. Before this, I preferred to straighten my hair with chemical relaxers and perms, or wear hair extensions, as was customary in the Caribbean. Being surrounded by beautiful Black women inspired me to embrace the natural parts of my body, including my kinky, and curly hair.

Then there was my prayer partner, Bianca, whose impromptu prayer circles kept me sane. Bianca was a cool, calm, and collected sweetheart from California who made friends with practically everybody. She embodied the spirit of the movie, Love and Basketball, and even with her 5-foot-2 frame, she could outplay most of the 6-foot-tall guys in our class at a game of hoops. Bianca was my sister in Christ, the one I called on frequently while at Howard when I needed to pray before major exams or major decision-making.

In medical school, I continued to excel in my coursework, though this was the most rigorous level of education I had experienced. My first year consisted mostly of dense and comprehensive biochemical lectures with assigned readings and reviews of clinical cases within our assigned small groups. We received tons of PowerPoint presentations to review, chapters to read, material to cover, and an exam to study for every two weeks. There was non-stop studying for exams and the information was so extensive that it literally reminded me of a scene where someone opens a fire hydrant and asks you to say, 'Aaaah'. God graced me, however, with the background I had with taking upper-level biology classes two years prior at Drexel, I continued earning excellent grades.

By the second year of medical school, I was already at the top of my class and many of my classmates found this out suddenly during one of our annual award ceremonies. I felt a sense of love and respect as I grew to appreciate my peers and hold them in high regard. Honestly, I believe they felt the same about me. Not only were my grades blessed and my relationship with my classmates an answer to a prayer, but I also continued to feel the intimate pulling of the Lord. One activity I started doing was printing scriptures on decorated sheets of paper and hanging them on my wall as a reminder to keep the word of God in my heart. What's more, in the spring of our second year, I decided to get baptized and several of my classmates attended this ceremony. I vividly remember during this same year, world-renowned evangelist and author, Dr. Myles Munroe, (who was also from The Bahamas) came to speak at my local church at Jesus House DC. I had an anatomy exam the next day that I was preparing for, but when I heard Dr. Myles Munroe would be coming to my church, I dropped all I was doing to go meet him.

He preached about the power of oneness before and after marriage and his famous phrase, 'Would you marry you?' reverberated in the building. After service, I went up to him trembling as I was so honored to finally meet him in person. With the brightest smile, Dr. Munroe encouraged me to stop shaking. He congratulated me on my academic accomplishments, and he cheerfully agreed to take a photo with me. He died in a plane crash just seven months later in The Bahamas. Like the entire world, I was beyond devastated and deeply shocked at this horrifying news.

Figure 8 *- Gina meeting Dr. Myles Munroe at Jesus House D.C church (April 2014)*

Moments like these often remind me to seize the opportunities we are given in life and to cherish the people around us because we truly do not know if that will be our last time with them. I am thankful that I got the opportunity to meet Dr. Myles Munroe before he left this earth. His legacy profoundly lives on.

After my second year of medical school, I prepared for the United States Medical Licensing Examination (USMLE), Step 1. This board exam is a standardized test that all medical students take on a national level that determines our career trajectory. The USMLE is a scored timed test. Students considering specific specialties, such as dermatology, surgery, emergency medicine, etc., were required to achieve higher performance scores to become eligible for their residency. We also had to pass this USMLE Step 1 exam to matriculate to the 3rd year of medical school, and ultimately, students who did not qualify could not continue their medical school journey. Test-taking in medical school was never-ending.

I always knew that I wanted to be a primary care doctor, specializing in family medicine because this was generalized, but impactful. I had a love for all things science and the thought of being able to treat babies, pregnant women, and the elderly made my heart smile.

116

I loved connecting with people and fostering relationships with a broad spectrum of patients mattered to me. Because of my high performance in school, many of my classmates were shocked that I wanted to become a primary care doctor rather than focusing on surgery or a higher-paying specialty. Regardless, I knew my gifts and felt the calling to focus on the preventative, firsthand treatment of my patients rather than chasing after money and prestige.

During the summer, my studying for Step 1 consisted of an intense 8-week schedule. I got up at 6 a.m. to read the Bible, then from 7 a.m. – 7 p.m. I reviewed my notes from the First Aid book, topic by topic - cardiology (heart), gastroenterology (gut), pulmonology (lungs), dermatology (skin), hematology (blood), and nephrology (kidneys) one week at a time. It was not long into my Step 1 studying that a sharp, shooting pain took over the left side of my head. Sadly, my migraines returned due to my non-stop studying. It got to a point where I took Excedrin for Migraine in advance for a month to complete my study schedule. Some days the pills worked and other days, it did not.

One day, while studying for my USMLE Step 1 I felt a nudge to pray. I closed all my study materials, which seemed so counterintuitive at the time as we were all on a tight study schedule reviewing the topics before our big test day. While quiet before the Lord in prayer, He took me to Ephesians 4, which I read entirely. By the time I got to the final two verses (v. 31-32), which urged the readers to get rid of all bitterness and to be kind to one another, I broke down and wept.

31 Get rid of all bitterness, rage and anger, brawling and slander, along with every form of malice. 32 Be kind and compassionate to one another, forgiving each other, just as in Christ God forgave you.
Ephesians 4:31-32 NIV [1]

Immediately, I thought about my ex-boyfriend Neo, whom I had not spoken to since senior year of college when I received that dreaded text message informing me that he had a baby on the way the weekend after we messed around. I felt the Lord leading me to release this bitterness I had buried for years so I called Neo on an international calling card from D.C, as he was still living in The Bahamas. He answered the call on the second ring. Nervously I said, "Hey, I want to apologize for being so angry at you for so long and for blocking you out of my life". Neo expressed that I did not owe him an apology and shared remorse for his part in hurting me and we agreed that we were simply too immature to have been involved with one another and as a result, we tainted a real childhood friendship.

Within minutes, something supernatural began to happen. Right there on the floor in my bedroom, I started having repeated jolts in my stomach with phrases and prompts that God was telling me to write down. These came in the form of warnings, reprimands, inspirations, and remarks around love, faith, my childhood abuse, relationships, and sexual purity. This went on for 6-8 weeks in the summer of 2015 and at the end, I had about 193 prompts written down in a notebook. I heard the audible instructions to share these on my social media pages, which were deactivated while I was studying for the Step 1 exam. Naturally, I was hesitant to carry out this instruction. I was a medical student within the top ranks of my class, and I did not want to look foolish to those around me. Yet, the more I suppressed sharing these prompts, the more jolts came rushing through not just my stomach, but my entire body.

At the age of 24, shortly after I took my USMLE exam, (which I passed), I began to courageously post these prompts on social media, sharing my testimony of how the Lord had turned my life around and encouraging fellow believers to walk in alignment with His word (See an excerpt below Figure 9).

Figure 9 - *An excerpt from an Instagram post July, 2015:*

"144. One of my ex-boyfriends was stimulating parts of my body I did not know existed with his hands. As a result, I struggled with masturbation for 3 years after being with him. Granted, it was me who continued to do it, but he helped to introduce me to it. These 3 years were time I could have spent growing in Christ, but I wanted more pleasure for myself. Truth is, it was a waste of time because I always wanted more & never felt satisfied. That boy would never understand how much that relationship stagnated my spiritual life. Smh. That's why it's so

important for we as young people to be mindful of who we allow into our intimate space. If your boo is not pointing you to Christ, please start asking yourself who sent him/her?... Seeing as how yall know all my business by now, let's earnestly talk: How is masturbation bringing Glory to God? When you masturbate, are you thinking about the sex you use to have? Are you rehearsing sex with your future husband/wife? Are you reenacting the porn you just watched or doing it while you watch porn? Better yet, are you listening to "slow songs" to get you in the "mood" (which, btw these songs are simply feeding the lustful Spirit within you & motivating you to sin)? Let's face facts, masturbation separates you from God because it feeds your flesh. It takes you 2 steps back, especially if you are doing this & you're saved... "Jesus replied, "No one who puts a hand to the plow and looks back is fit for service in the kingdom of God." (Luke 9:62). Let it go Kings & Queens! Wait on the Lord to send you your spouse where it's completely legal to participate in sexual activities with your husband/wife. If you need help until then, please seek out a trusted friend, mentor, or pastor for accountability. Prayer brought me out. What you shame for? "Woe to the world because of the things that cause people to stumble! Such things must come, but woe to the person through whom they come! If your hand or your foot causes you to stumble, cut it off and throw it away. It is better for you to enter life maimed or crippled than to have two hands or two feet and be thrown into eternal fire. (Matthew 18:7-9)" #captivesbesetfree"

I was indeed zealous and blunt with my approach in advocating for sexual purity, and holiness. For the first time, I shared publicly that I had been sexually molested as a child. There were countless whispers about my sanity throughout campus after these posts were shared. Many of those I considered friends, as well as people from my own family and hometown, condemned me. *'She belongs to a cult,'* one said. *'G, are you okay? Where are you going with this fake Facebook prophet act?'* asked another. *'Did you read all that foolishness Gina is posting online?'* someone else chimed in. *She's lost it!"* thought most, unanimously. These were the comments that followed in multiple group chats.

Still, I felt freedom for being obedient to the Lord's instructions and following through on what He told me to do. It was a rush of fear and security all in one, which I had never experienced before. I was openly declaring my belief and allegiance to Jesus Christ, which at that time, had been a solid foundation for me. Next came third year of medical school.

During my third year, we moved from being in classrooms and lecture halls to seeing actual patients face-to-face in the form of 'rotations'. Rotations were where we went to the hospital or clinic to evaluate patients in person and then present our findings, along with a plan to our Attending, who was a licensed physician and our instructor. We rotated through family medicine, obstetrics and gynecology (OBGYN), pediatrics, surgery, internal medicine, neurology, etc. We also took a shelf exam at the end of every rotation, specific to each specialty. It was during this year of medical school that I began to feel the most exhausted with studying. Some rotations like surgery required us to be up at 4:30 a.m. to make it to the hospital by 5 a.m., and sometimes we did not get out of the hospital until after 7 p.m. My energy to study once I got home was slim. For the first time, being the highest performer in my class began to lose its appeal. I studied the material as best as I could with the energy that I had left, totally unattached to the outcome. Even still, during my junior year at Howard University, I was inducted into the Alpha Omega Alpha (AOA) Honor Society, an award given to those in the top 7% of their medical school class.

Rotations were evermore eye-opening and transformational because I got to work with beautiful Black male and female doctors who were my attendings. For instance, there was a strong and brilliant pediatrician, Dr. Forrester from Trinidad, who had a distinct style of teaching which reminded me of my own mother. I had a resilient African American female Attending, Dr. White-Coleman, who taught me during my internal medicine rotation. At the time, she was recovering from brain tumor surgery. She had a slight left-sided facial droop but was determined to show up for her patients. She later died from this illness in 2019. My family medicine Attending, Dr. Filani, was the head of the department and a young adult leader at my church, Jesus House DC. Black excellence coupled with humanity, style, and grace embodied my instructors and I felt so empowered in my brilliance by being surrounded and taught by them.

Graciously, my extracurricular activities also prospered at Howard including being President of our Family Medicine interest group, President of our Christian Medical & Dental Association, going on a mission trip to Haiti with an incredible group of doctors and volunteers, and winning countless scholarships and awards for my commitment to service, leadership, and excellence. By the time my final year of medical school came in 2016, I was applying to some of the top Family Medicine Residency programs across the United States. I achieved higher scores on part 2 of the USMLE standardized test (Step 2) while making time for fun with my classmates such as traveling to Trinidad and Tobago and experiencing their beautiful culture of carnival. Though I did not graduate as the top student in medical school, the accolades still came in the form of other service and leadership awards on graduation day.

I did not have much time for boys while in medical school though there were a couple of potential love interests during my latter years, which did not make it far.

Howard University was everything I needed and then some. I discovered more of myself in this environment and made lifelong friendships with future Black doctors from all walks of life. It was a blessing to be surrounded by such excellence and camaraderie each day and I left D.C. with a sense of hope and pride in who I was and greater intimacy with Christ. It was evident to me that I was more than my grades at Howard. I was loved and celebrated, not just for these achievements but also for my altruistic service to my community, my genuine love for my peers, and a cherished and honest love for God's word. Slowly, the layers of childhood trauma were being unearthed, but I was just scratching the surface.

V. Lessons

- There is beauty on the other side of you enduring through seasons of rejection and pain.

- The journey to medical school is hard, but the experiences and friends you meet along the way help to shape your character, passion, and worldview.

- Continue building healthy friendships and mentorship in medical school.

- Seek out scholarships and donors to help fund medical school.

- Have wholesome fun. You are studying hard, don't forget to have fun.

- Don't stop believing in yourself and your WHY while in the grind of pursuing higher education.

- Being black is beautiful and worthy of being celebrated. We are far more than what the media and stereotypes try to paint us as.

- Cherish the excellent people and friends that you make along the journey by being good to people and respecting the value they add to your life. These could very well be your lifelong friends.

- Take time to reflect on who you are and the type of professional you hope to be one day. Get clear about your values, interests, and talents.

- Don't be afraid to take risks. Travel, even while in school. The world is truly your oyster.

- Do not disqualify yourself or lose sight of your excellence.

Chapter VI

Residency -
Call me Dr. Gi

Figure 10 - *Dr. Guillaume and her mother standing by the Howard University College of Medicine sign on Match Day in her long white coat (March 2017)*

Toward the end of medical school, after third-year rotations, students declare which specialty they wish to apply for. This next phase known as 'Residency' is the final step before one can be an independent, licensed, and practicing medical doctor. Residency is where medical school graduates are further trained in a rigorous hospital setting as the acting doctor in the specific specialty that they chose for a period of 3-8 more years. The sacrifices and time dedicated to becoming a medical doctor are truly endless. After rotations, I was still convinced that family medicine was my specialty of calling. Starting the fall of my 4th year of medical school, I applied through the national Electronic Residency Application Service (ERAS) and for the next 3-6 months, interviewed at the institutions that offered me a visit.

I applied to about twenty Family Medicine Residency programs across the U.S. and interviewed at fourteen of these hospital training sites. During this process, I took out an additional Sallie Mae private loan to cover expenses (e.g., airfare, gas, hotel stays, and interview clothing) while applying for Residency. Some programs provided lodging and depending on the state, I sometimes spent the night with a friend from college to save money. It was around this time that my migraines returned with a vengeance. The Excedrin that once worked for me in college and while I was studying did not even touch my headaches now. There were times when I got a migraine while I was out with friends and had to sit in my car and sleep it off in the parking garage before I could drive myself home. Enough was enough—I finally reached out to the Student Health Center at Howard, where I was referred to a Neurologist for further evaluation. My Neurologist ordered an MRI where I lay on a table in a noisy tube machine for an hour while the radiologist examined my brain. Thankfully, my results were normal and nothing was found on my brain. It was recommended that I do physical therapy to help loosen up my neck muscles. The frequent studying, busyness with travel, and ten years of non-stop grind were impacting my body. These were additional sacrifices that occurred in my pursuit of becoming Dr. Guillaume.

Residency, however, was the ultimate sacrifice. This next step after medical school was the process of being assigned as a doctor in a hospital or clinic setting, seeing patients who were ill and placing orders for them. This was a time for hands-on experience in the specialty of your choice which lasted for about three years for general specialties such as family medicine or pediatrics, four years for specialties such as emergency medicine or neurology specialties, six years for surgery, or eight years for neurosurgery or cardiothoracic surgery.

My friends from Howard researched programs on a platform called Doximity. They shared that the top family medicine programs were on the West Coast and encouraged me to apply to programs there. I was nervous to live that far away from my family, but being an adventurous person at heart, I ultimately decided to go, to at least see for myself. Gallantly, I applied for and interviewed for six residency programs in the state of California and immediately fell in love with the location. On the interview trail to the West Coast, the sight of palm trees and the occasional scent of marijuana hit me as I stepped off the plane at the Burbank Airport with the cool breeze of the Pacific Ocean reminding me somewhat of The Bahamas. 'To live and die in LA' by Tupac was also on repeat on 93.1 FM as I drove through Southern California in my rental car.

During my week of interviews while hopping from one hospital to the next, one program captured my heart - Harbor UCLA Medical Center. The Program

Director at the time, Dr. Castro, presented on the impact of a social justice-driven residency providing care for some of the poorest patients in L.A. County. Harbor UCLA Medical Center saw patients who were usually turned away from other private hospitals in Los Angeles County. It was a safety net hospital that frequently treated the uninsured. Their Residents were equally diverse with their many brown and black faces in the heart of Southern California giving them an attractive flare.

The other programs that stood out were Tufts Family Medicine in Boston, MA which had a large Haitian population along with a 4-year Family Medicine Residency in Lawrence, MA. Ultimately, location, patient demographic, weather, and community involvement played a major factor in my decision on where to go for residency. Furthermore, I was also applying to programs, during an intense election year (2016), in which Donald Trump became the President of the United States. With palpable racial tensions in the air, I was cautious about where I applied for residency as a black woman.

With prayer and consideration, I ranked Harbor UCLA #1 on my list. On 'Match Day' at Howard University in March 2017, I opened my envelope and was pleased to learn that they ranked me high as well. I was going to Los Angeles, California for the next three years to complete my Residency in Family Medicine. My mother, my best friend Ebony, and her mother stood on that stage on Match Day with visible emotions as I received my long white coat as Dr. Guillaume. I was a graduate of Howard University headed to Los Angeles for Residency.

Before starting the next chapter as the newly minted, Dr. Guillaume, I spent the summer after medical school in The Bahamas with my family and friends. This time, I could feel the love and respect of the people in my hometown. It was not often that a doctor came from our settlement of Jones Town in Eight Mile Rock. To watch the smile on Mammy's (my mom) and Mr. Baba's (my dad) faces was inexpressible. We were in a state of gratitude, joy, and honor. Yet, no positive state of mind could prepare me for the next three years of my life.

I went 'back to Cali' like Biggie Smalls said at the end of the summer of 2017 to start my orientation for Residency—and like Biggie Smalls, a part of me died in LA. The list of paperwork, background checks, and modules was endless, and the scrambling felt never-ending. Thankfully, our program gave us a 2-week orientation before starting work in the hospital for our Residency cohort to bond. I embarked alongside eleven brave souls who were all newly crowned MDs on this Family Medicine Residency Journey for the next 3 years of our lives.

Residency was truly an art of warfare. We fought to keep our eyes open after working 80 hours per week with minimal days off. We armed ourselves until our next day off, which in fact, could be three weeks apart. Residents were allowed only four days off a month and legally, this could mean working three weeks without a day off as long as you had a stretch of four consecutive days off within a 28-day period. My schedule as a first-year resident also known as an 'Intern Year' consisted of heavy inpatient rotations which meant working inside the hospital either seeing patients from the Emergency Room or following our patients once they were admitted to a room inside the hospital.

As Interns, we were assigned to a team of 2nd or 3rd-year residents who were known as our 'Seniors'— collectively, we were supervised by an attending (an independent, licensed, Board-certified practicing doctor). Interns were among the first to see patients who were ill, get a good history of their symptoms, do a thorough physical exam, come up with a treatment plan, and run that plan by our Senior. We also placed orders for medications to be administered, IV bags to be hung, and communicated with the nursing staff to close the loop.

Then there were pagers. We also carried pagers where nursing staff and specialty providers could contact us with their questions or requests on demand. I hated my pager! The sound of it beeping still haunts me today. I honestly do not know how I survived my intern year. The cheerful, spirit-filled person who left Howard University soon felt like a robotic zombie, high on coffee and prayers. I often went to the hospital's call room to spend the night after only 1-2 hours of sleep because I was too exhausted to drive home, or I would chew on a stick of gum to help me stay awake while driving back to my apartment.

For the curious, Intern rotations consisted of trauma surgery, internal medicine, family medicine inpatient, NICU (neonatal intensive care unit), pediatrics inpatient, adult ICU (intensive care unit), and CCU (Cardiac care unit). We were responsible for caring for up to ten patients, typically with their information (a.k.a. Handoff sheets) attached to our hips. By 6 a.m., we checked into the hospital to receive Sign-out Forms from the covering Night Shift Intern, where we learned about any major incidents that happened with our patient overnight. Interns then went from room to room examining our patients and communicating with the nurses, sharing relevant updates. We then placed orders for blood draws and labs, checked on test results that may have come back that morning, and read any updated notes from specialists who were also following our patients.

In an orbit, we then debriefed about our patients in the physician cafeteria with our Senior Residents over breakfast. Next in the galaxy, we made 'rounds' with our Attending before lunch who often asked us to adjust our treatment plans for the patient that day and used this time to teach us. The remainder of our universe consisted of responding to requests and/or placing orders made by our patients, nurses, or specialists. We often had new patients come into the Emergency room (ER) to evaluate and admit who would then be added to our roster. Typically, around 6 p.m. we passed on the Sign-out forms to the night person, sharing information about incidents that may have happened with our patients during the day. Sometimes, in this vortex, if we were the "on-call" intern, we spent the entire 24-hour period in the hospital, repeating our daily routines at night with minimal rest. Interns were literally in the twilight zone. [Note: Each residency program has its own on-call and shift schedules].

In residency, I treated all sorts of conditions from heart attacks and heart failure, diabetic skin infections, childhood asthma, COPD exacerbations, kidney infections, STDs and HIV-related complications, premature labor, and many more. I also saw men and women take their last breath—dying in my arms after their hearts stopped beating, even after we performed CPR on them. These were the worst days. Witnessing a body become inanimate in real-time, then having to perform a death 'exam' was otherworldly, in and of itself. A wave of sadness and somberness overtook the room and the expectation of stoicism as I fought back tears required restraint. In those moments I was undoubtedly reminded how short and fragile one's life is. The first time I witnessed a patient's death was during my first year as an Intern when her heart stopped during an interventional radiology procedure. A hospital wide code was called during this procedure and our internal medicine inpatient code team rushed to her bedside taking turns pressing down on her chest, praying and hoping that her pulse would return. Medications were pumped through her veins at the same time as the leading Resident kept a close eye on her heart monitor screen. Despite our best efforts, she did not survive. Her pulse stopped and her heart monitor remained flat lined. After the time of death was declared and the senior Resident stayed to complete her death certificate, I rushed to the restroom, closed the stall behind me, and wept. Residency, indeed, was like walking through a tornado wearing scrubs and a packed white coat with nothing but adrenaline and coffee as fuel. Thankfully, God kept me.

I worked well with my co-residents, and we enjoyed each other's company outside of the hospital. My co-interns were a diverse mix of Asian, White, and Brown faces. I was the only Black intern in my class. We kept sane by hosting potlucks, housewarmings, movie nights, going on hikes, and celebrating each other's birthdays and baby showers. We were all in this struggle together fighting the war of fatigue, all while we delivered quality care to those who needed it most. I continued going to church on Sundays when I wasn't working, though this was rare. My best friend Ebony had mentioned this young, vibrant, and spirited church in Northern Los Angeles called, One LA led by Pastor Touré Roberts and his wife Pastor Sarah Jakes Roberts. Church often had the ability to infuse my soul especially when I felt like I was hanging on by a thread. Their co-pastor, at that time, Stephanie Ike also resonated with me given her Nigerian background and gracious delivery of the truth of God's word and his essence. I was grateful to have some footing during this tiring time of my life.

Harbor UCLA Residency also paired each intern with a faculty advisor who met with us periodically to check in on our progress throughout our journey. I was grateful that I was paired with a loving and God-fearing Chinese advisor, Dr. Liu, who consistently prayed with me and for me during residency. Dr. Liu sometimes invited me for walks or dinner, which she paid for (Hallelujah because I was a broke intern). She helped me to stay grounded while practicing medicine at a high-stakes and stressful pace and often recommended that I focus on my end goal. Dr. Liu's specialty was geriatrics and she ran the nursing home rotation during our residency. She was truly an anchor for me during this period.

And yet, the saga continued. The beautiful thing about Howard was that I made friends from all over the globe who became my friends for life. We had two 2-weeks vacations per year, and I was ecstatic to take one of them during mid-intern year. I visited a friend from medical school who lived in Dallas, Texas. At that time, she was starting her internal medicine residency there. On this trip, I posted a story on social media that captured the attention of one of my medical school classmates— we'll call him Felix. Felix was also a first-generation doctor whose family was from Nigeria. He complimented and flirted with me a few times at Howard, but I always found him to be too flashy for my taste. Felix invited me and my friend over to Houston to see him for the weekend. We agreed and my friend and I took the 4-hour drive from Dallas to Houston to meet up with him. Felix had rented a high-rise apartment through Airbnb for us, which was absolutely gorgeous! He took us to a Nigerian party and paid for us to see the movie Black Panther that weekend.

While out at the Nigerian party, we drank, danced, and had a good time. It felt great to forget about the stressful twilight zone of my residency and enjoy the atmosphere of good food and friends. Out of the blue, Felix pulled me onto the dance floor. However, what started as an innocent dance between us then turned into him reaching in for a kiss. We made out at the party, which eventually rolled over to the Airbnb stay. That night, one thing led to another, and Felix and I became very intimate. This was the second time I received oral sex from a man. At first, it was a welcomed release, given the hectic pace of my residency, but the guilt soon crept in. Didn't I promise God to remain a virgin until I was married? Ugh. Felix was attempting to have full intercourse that night, but I declined because that promise haunted me even while slipping.

Shortly after my return to L.A., it got awkward. Felix asked me to reimburse him for the movie ticket. I paid him, then graciously blocked him. After engaging so intimately with a man, it did not feel good for this to be the result, but I counted my losses and pressed forward. This was a moment of weakness that was amplified by the perfect storm of stress, partying, and alcohol. For the next couple of months, I sincerely felt the guilt and shame of giving in so quickly. I was embarrassed that old habits were still creeping into my life, even as a Resident doctor. Yes, even as a Resident doctor slip-ups still occurred during my walk with Christ.

I share this vulnerable moment with transparency as a reminder that no matter how high you rise, it is still possible to stumble, especially during seasons of high demands and when placing yourself in environments that trigger old habits. The guilt that followed this incident was excruciating for me and easily made me doubt my connection to the Lord. On the contrary, this guilt is a sign of conviction, shedding a beautiful light on one's closeness to the instructions and will of the Lord that you serve. It is the feeling of having grieved someone we love—a grief that exists because the One we have grieved is real and truly exists. Indeed, it was very easy to wallow in self-pity, and believe me, I did. I cried, I journaled, I confessed my sin to the Lord, and I cried some more. Eventually, I viewed this mistake as an invitation to be more vigilant and to move forward, believing that this was a temporary setback, not a permanent residence. I blocked Felix and moved forward with the work I had to get back to.

Toward the end of my intern year, we took another USMLE exam Step 3 standardized test, which I performed well on. Though our schedule felt suffocating, we were learning so much from the hands-on experience of Residency. During the second year of residency, we had more outpatient rotations, which meant seeing patients who were coming into the clinic for more routine and acute follow-up instead of in-hospital, emergency care -i.e. inpatient observations like during Intern year. Being in the clinic was more in my element. I enjoyed the slower pace of talking to my patients about their concerns, examining them in our sunlit exam rooms, going to the precepting room to sit down with my Attending, and reviewing my plans with the instructor.

Some clinic days were certainly busier than others, but I learned so much from my patients, receiving feedback from my Attending, and looking up evidence-based guidelines. What I was not as prepared for was the additional paperwork, charting of notes, and messages that came through the electronic health record for the patients I took care of in the clinic. We still rotated through inpatient specialties at the hospital, but this time I was in a more 'Senior' role, which afforded me the space to gain knowledge as a supervisor.

As time went on, I grew more and more fatigued. Many of my patients were either not taking their medication, or they were not taking them as prescribed, which impacted their diabetes and blood pressure readings. My Spanish was also minimal, so I used the interpreter phone with many of my patients. This pushed my appointment times beyond the typical fifteen minutes I was assigned to see them, which meant that I was often behind. It was common to have to write 8-10 notes at the end of the afternoon, sign papers from my mailbox, along with staring at several messages in my inbox that needed attention. Most nights, it was common to go home after 8 p.m. feeling exhausted and malnourished because I ate whatever was available—sometimes not at all, due to the busyness of my schedule. Practicing medicine began to feel more like a chore than my calling and ironically, the unhealthiest I had ever been, even while I was treating those who were sick. My spare time consisted mostly of taking naps and drinking lots of caffeine. I also felt as if I had no time to date. However, I watched my peers get married, start families, and buy homes. I started to feel discontent.

Of course, my migraines returned in the middle of my Residency, which further added to my life's stress. This time, I decided to try something new—acupuncture. A Neurologist I spoke to recommended I give acupuncture a try and at that point in my life, I was willing to try anything to get these migraines to cease. Since I found openings in my schedule during the second year of my Residency, I booked acupuncture sessions once a week with a petite Asian lady in my neighborhood. My Acupuncturist immediately confirmed that I was stressed based on the tightness of my muscles and my heavy breathing. "You work a very stressful job, huh?" she asked, to which I hung my head down and responded "Yes". The first four sessions were scary and painful because I was not accustomed to needles being embedded into sensitive parts of my body, such as my forehead, ears, and even my stomach, but it worked. The lasting results of acupuncture were well worth the pain, as I did not have migraines for years afterward. I was grateful for the acupuncture sessions, as they undoubtedly helped me to continue my pursuit of becoming Dr. Guillaume.

When I wasn't working on Sundays, I was able to attend church more regularly. I learned more about our first lady, Sarah Jakes Roberts, through her first book called Lost and Found where she shared her testimony of becoming pregnant as a young teenager and her failed marriage to a football player who often cheated on her. Shortly after, I came across a blog she wrote before her first book deal and thought, *Imagine that, she has a blog*. The idea of starting a blog to inspire hope and share my personal journey was unshakable. One night, as I was surfing the internet, I came across an ad for starting a blog. A beautiful wife and mother who blogged about her travel experiences with her family created the course and was offering to teach others how to do it. I wanted to take the course, but I was too broke and beat up to bother.

One night, as my third and final year of residency was approaching, I was on the phone with my best friend, Ebony, sharing stories of the perils of Residency. I told her I was exhausted from moving at such a fast pace. Yes, I was making a difference in the lives of my community, but I was also discontent that I had not started a relationship yet. I shared that I was thinking about starting a blog, but I did not know if I had the time to manage this while in residency. I was also still battling the guilt and shame I was feeling after my experience with Felix a few months prior. Thankfully, I also had a trusted confidante whom I could share my lapse in judgement with rather than keeping it all inside. Ebony spoke life into me and helped me to shake it off.

Do you know that my amazing best friend purchased the blogging course and gave it to me as a gift on my 28th birthday? She attempted to recover my soul, and truly, she did just that! During the start of my third and final year of residency, my schedule consisted of mostly outpatient clinics with 1-2 inpatient rotations, thus I had more time away from the hospital. In my spare time, I reviewed the course material and built my blog from scratch, little by little.

I went live with my blog in January 2019, near the end of my second year of residency and slowly I felt my pulse return to my zombie-walking body. About once a week on a Saturday or Sunday, I wrote blog posts about having faith, dealing with rejection, spiritual growth, navigating love and relationships, and simply sharing my testimony of childhood trauma. It was beautiful and I felt closer to the Lord again.

Interestingly enough, it was not until I intentionally drew closer to the Lord by faith that I felt alive again. Ironically, Residency and becoming Dr. Guillaume had not given me the internal satisfaction and fulfillment I imagined they would have. Though I enjoyed my patients and many of them were grateful to be treated by a Black doctor, the practice of medicine itself felt burdensome, like something was missing from my life. By the end of my residency, I seriously doubted whether I would stay in the profession. Only God could make it clear to me and show me the path I would take next.

VI. Lessons

♦ Residency is difficult. It's not you. It's the way the system is designed.

♦ Making time for self-care (i.e. exercise, therapy, sleep, hobbies, etc.) is necessary especially while in a high-stressed environment.

♦ Be vigilant and mindful of your triggers and weak points. I slipped sexually when I was stressed. More slip-ups occur in these settings as they are prime spaces for young adults to stumble.

♦ Do not go through residency alone. Reach out for help— with trusted friends and family who can pray for and encourage you.

♦ Ebony spoke life back into me at my lowest moments. The people you surround yourself with the most have a significant impact on your decisions, so choose your friends wisely.

♦ Locate mentors or colleagues in your field who can teach you how to manage your money as early as possible.

♦ Continue to pray and seek the face of Jesus in all the seasons of your life.

♦ Continue to pray about your purpose even while pursuing your career as these may not be the same. Ask God to make His plans plain and give you the faith to pursue your purpose.

Chapter VII

Fellowship

Figure 11- Dr. Guillaume 'Community Health Fellowship' photo announcement. Image taken by Truc Dinh, MD (Howard University College of Medicine classmate)

Finally, my third and final year of residency came! However, I was unsure if I wanted to remain in the profession. There were many career fairs hosted by my program. I considered moonlighting, which is where a licensed physician takes a paid position as a contractor at a clinic with open slots to help expand their knowledge and/or make extra money. I also heard about the possibility of doing LOCUMS, which is another temporary job that many physicians take, working shifts at their leisure. I was strongly considering staying in Southern California, but I was not sold on entering private practice as a full-time doctor because of the overwhelming paperwork and insurance-related burdens on top of seeing patients.

During my residency, there were specific faculty members who embodied social justice and advocacy including a husband and wife who worked at Harbor UCLA for 20+ years. This couple ran a pipeline program, which sought to recruit high school students and college graduates into the field of medicine. I applied for this pipeline program and got the opportunity to work with some energetic and enthusiastic students for six weeks at the beginning of my last year of Residency. Being surrounded by such fresh energy also helped to revitalize my love for medicine and my dedication to preventative health while providing quality care for the underserved. Residents assisting in the pipeline program gave lectures to students about their journey to medicine. Some of us shared our experiences of being first-generation college graduates and our passion for community service. We also covered topics such as food insecurity, food deserts, and redlining practices that kept marginalized communities confined to poverty and away from white neighborhoods. It was then that I realized what was missing within the four walls of the exam room—social determinants of health. It was clear that these environmental factors including a lack of food, shelter, safety, and in some cases lack of access to quality health care were negatively impacting the outcome of my patients who were the most ill. While I enjoyed offering medications as treatment for acute and chronic conditions, more work and involvement addressing the environment in which many of our patients lived needed to be done for more comprehensive and sustainable health outcomes.

Dr. Puvvula, a petite Indian powerhouse and the leading lady and wife of Dr. Granados who headed the pipeline program, naturally became one of my mentors. An opportunity came and was presented by Dr. Puvvula, to start a Community Health Fellowship at Harbor UCLA which intrigued me. A Fellowship is an extension of residency where graduating seniors continued for an additional year or two to gain more experience within a specific field rather than going into full independent practice as an attending. A Community Health Fellow would work with community-based organizations, precept residents in a clinic or inpatient setting, meet with a clinical advisor to develop community teaching projects and continue working within the pipeline program. Given my back and forth with taking on a full-time attending role after residency and my desire to address more of the social determinants of health impacting our population, I applied and eventually was accepted as the first Community Health Fellow in Family Medicine at Harbor UCLA for an additional year.

To the world's surprise, COVID-19 shut everything down around this time. My third year of residency ended with my class and I having to do virtual learning as the COVID-19 pandemic hit within the last quarter of our training, March 2020. Harbor UCLA saw its first patient with COVID-19 in the ICU who happened to be one of my patients at the clinic. The reality of being so isolated and having to always wear masks as a physician was brutal. Chaos ensued in hospitals across the United States. I watched as our hospital waiting room spaces were converted to makeshift patient rooms. Normal wards that were used to admit patients turned into ICU wards as the need for more ventilator machines rose in our hospital. Being a trainee in the hospital was a nightmare and further added to the exhaustion of healthcare workers universally.

On top of this matter, I watched the full video of George Floyd lying on a concrete pavement in Minnesota as a white police officer put his knee on his neck for 8 minutes and 46 seconds as he gasped the words heard all over the world, "I can't breathe." Within a matter of days, the year 2020 went from bad to worse as a series of national protests ensued leaving the air feeling thick and dense for Black people in America, many of us feeling as if we too were unable to breathe. I saw the face of my black nephew, a college student in Florida who looked like Michael Brown, the 18-year-old black teen who was gunned down in Ferguson, Missouri in 2014. Watching the video of George Floyd's murder, I also saw the face of my little brother who was living in Dallas, Texas, the same city where Botham Jean, the 26-year-old accountant of Haitian descent was murdered by a white police officer in his home as the officer entered the wrong apartment.

The year 2020 brought me to my knees mentally with intense paranoia for my family and myself. The emotional turmoil of anger and grief choked my hope for a brighter future in America. It became more difficult to wake up and put on my clothes to drive to the clinic. Every conversation I had with a non-black person felt fake and I grew more guarded. I triple-checked the door locks before going to bed at night. Even as medical doctors, the toll of racism still weighed heavily on black professionals and haunted us in the workplace. Yet, we still showed up daily with poised expressions, carrying the duality of triumph and pain.

I needed help and for the first time in my life of almost 30 years, I began researching mental health therapists near me. At first, I went through my health insurance at the time as a resident and searched specifically for a Black therapist. There were also websites like psychologytoday.com where you could search for a mental health therapist by location and contact them based on whether they accepted your insurance or offered self-pay options. Initially, I spoke with a black male therapist, but this was not the right fit as he began to discuss his politics in the sessions. At times, I could not decipher if the therapy sessions were for me or him. Eventually, I found a white behavioralist in my Residency program who provided clarity on the racial trauma my body was experiencing. Through ongoing talk therapy, she helped me to realize that I was not only mourning the lack of safety I was exposed to as a black person in America, but also the feelings of being discriminated against as a little Haitian girl growing up in The Bahamas. From that moment, I continued to seek mental health therapy in each season of my life which helped me process the heavy mental load that had accumulated throughout my life. As I started this journey through mental self-care, my only regret was that I did not begin therapy sooner.

My residency ended with national racial trauma, a global pandemic, and a heavily charged election period. Our final board certification exam was pushed back, which gave me and my peers more time to study. *Did I mention the exams did not stop?* Thankfully, we all passed with flying colors. Our graduation ceremony at the end of residency training, was smaller than usual due to the global pandemic and sadly, my friends and family could not travel from The Bahamas to Southern California to attend the celebration. Nevertheless, in July 2020, I was gearing up for the next chapter of my career as a Community Health Fellow while many of my classmates took on full-time outpatient attending positions, addiction medicine fellowship opportunities, and LOCUMS.

God continued to meet me. As the newly minted Community Health Fellow at Harbor UCLA Medical Center, I led many of the organization's activities, such as the Pipeline program, where we mentored another round of high school and premed students. Many of these same students successfully passed the MCAT exam and are now first-generation doctors as well. Since we usually spoke openly about the impact of racism on health care, I quickly became a health equity advocate at our hospital.

For instance, I was a panelist at a Black Lives Matter event, discussing why Black people were hesitant to take the COVID-19 vaccine. Through this humbling opportunity, I was able to hear experiences confirming why Black people felt a sense of distrust with the healthcare system in the United States. The host shared how she almost died during childbirth, while another panelist, a leader in the Muslim community, vehemently rebuked vaccination. Even though these types of conversations and interactions are not taught in medical school, our patients have these types of experiences daily. During my Community Health Fellowship, I was able to bridge this gap and educate resident physicians and attendings about the history of medical racism and how to approach marginalized populations, especially surrounding healthcare.

Notably, my fellowship also allowed me to lead a clinic-wide Black History Month newsletter, and I gave several roundtable-style lectures about health inequity to our hospital staff. I also presented on this topic at national American Family Medicine conferences (virtually, in the setting of COVID-19), and mobilized a group of Brown and Black resident physicians to give accurate information about the COVID-19 vaccine to those who had questions or concerns in our community. Similarly, in my fellowship, I worked with our emergency room department in collaboration with the American Heart Association to help distribute fresh fruits and vegetables to our underserved community once a week. My love for humanity and heart for service was expanded through this fellowship opportunity and I regained my love and passion for the field of medicine once again.

It also helped that my fellowship consisted of mostly outpatient clinics without calls, where I continued to see patients in the clinic setting and served as a preceptor to residents, teaching them and giving feedback on their treatment plans for patients they saw in the outpatient setting. I now had more weekends to exercise, blog, rest, and rejuvenate. My passion for education was also elevated as I worked with a group of residents to develop primary care cards to help them remember evidence-based care while in the clinic. Another gem of this season was delving deeper into Adverse Childhood Experiences (ACEs), which is a set of trauma a child experiences before their 18th birthday including childhood physical, sexual, and emotional abuse; child neglect; mental illness and depression; having a suicidal, drug-addicted, or an alcoholic family member in the home; and witnessing domestic violence against a mother. ACEs, I learned, greatly impacted the health outcomes of children and adults in primary care, putting them at increased risk of the leading causes of death in America. Dr. Nadine Burke Harris was the California Surgeon General at the time, who pioneered ACEs research in northern California. I was able to present alongside two other faculty members to our Family Medicine Residents in this Fellowship about ACEs and toxic stress.

I watched God enlarge my capacity for the things I loved at a pace that was more manageable while gaining clinical experience and a heart for the community in the process. I intended to stay in California after my residency to work in a clinic that would allow me time to focus on health equity and community-based work. Specifically, I had my eyes set on the Martin Luther King Jr. Hospital and its affiliates in L.A., but God had other plans.

As the Community Health Fellowship was coming to an end, in mid-January of 2021, I received an email from Cindy, another resident who was nearing the end of her Emergency Medicine Residency. Cindy shared a job listing from a local community health center in Portland, Oregon that was founded by a Black pastor and a Jewish doctor in 2006. They were looking for their first Black medical director. I looked at the application and researched the center which had many Black staff and served a large Black population. It was the only clinic in Oregon devoted to Black health. I was captivated by this clinic and the role but dismissed it because of the location. They were looking for someone with two years of experience post-residency and I only had one year of experience. Cindy quickly assured me, "Girl, the world is your oyster. Do not limit yourself. If you take on this role, I know you would be good at it. Don't sell yourself short." I thanked Cindy for her kind words and prayed about my decision.

Around this time, I was participating in a Bible course called, Everyday Seminary, which provided a more in-depth way to study the Bible and apply Biblical principles to our lives. We were already six weeks into the program and were in the chapter about Godly decision-making, which involved seeking out God's will over our own, backed by the word of God. I took this as a sign to at least investigate. Thus, I shared the job listing with my mentor, Dr. Puvvula who agreed that I was crazy for looking at a job in Portland, Oregon, but also agreed that based on the role and responsibilities I would be a perfect fit for this organization.

As such, I prayed and prayed some more. I prayed in the morning. I prayed at lunchtime, and I prayed at night. I went through old journals and leadership assignments I wrote at Drexel University, which reminded me of the grace of leadership that God had placed over my life. I dedicated time to my application for the Medical Director position and even shared my love for Jesus in my Personal Statement, which was rare to do in medicine. Speaking about Jesus could be a touchy subject amongst intellectuals and professionals who are trained to think logically in an evidence-based framework. Sharing one's faith while in the medical field can sometimes feel compartmentalized to 'faith-based' health centers and non-profits. I finally felt like I could present my whole self to an organization based on the story of the clinic's founding women.

In January 2021, I submitted my application and heard back from the center that same day. There were a series of phone calls and emails between the founding physician and me, followed by in-person interviews, which solidified that I was a perfect fit for the center.

The interview week to the center in Oregon was surreal. I stayed in this quaint Airbnb offered by the center and explored the "Rose City" in the Spring. The center itself was a beautiful, brick-orange, two-story building with the heart to match. From the moment I walked in, I was greeted with Black artwork from the South and classic black-and-white photos of native Portlanders adorning the walls. Quotes and portraits of Martin Luther King Jr. and Barack Obama lined the hallways accentuating the two exam rooms and single lab space the clinic offered. There was palpable history, beauty, and regality in the air. My favorite were the staff members who were mostly a group of beautiful Black women who clearly loved what they did.

The center was run by the co-founding Jewish doctor and a well-organized white executive director who reported to a Board of predominantly Black professionals with a long-standing history of serving the Portland community. Everyone was so welcoming and hospitable—they clearly wanted me there and the more I learned about the organization's legacy, the more I felt like this was certainly a dream come true. The opportunity to lead a clinic, serve Black patients, and be surrounded by like-minded community made the thought of living in Portland, Oregon worthwhile. It seemed like this was a perfectly sized glove that fit my hand—divinely.

In March 2021, at the end of the interview week I fell in love with the nature of Oregon state. I was offered the position before returning to California to complete my Community Medicine Fellowship. I cried tears of joy and stood in disbelief at the noticeable hand of God on my life.

I, Gina Guillaume, a young girl from the hood, who was sexually abused, struggled with low self-esteem and endured treacherous experiences with men, was not only blessed to attend college, complete a master's degree, finish medical school after facing rejection, and earned my Family Medicine Board Certification, was chosen to be the first Black Medical Director of a local health center at the age of thirty-one. I arrived to Portland, Oregon, in November 2021, starry-eyed, purpose-filled, and ready to take the world by storm.

I am living proof that God exists. He takes care of his children no matter our upbringing, trauma, socioeconomic status, or pitfalls. If we continue to walk with God, he will continue to walk with us. Do not be afraid to pursue your dreams, even if you have slip-ups and missteps along the way. We have a good heavenly father who can pick us up and wipe away our shame. I hope my story inspires you to keep moving on as you are. Soon enough, God will reintroduce you to the champion he created you to be.

VII. Lessons

- God will provide.

- Depending on your goals, it is okay to seek out fellowship opportunities before entering private practice after completing your residency experience.

- No matter your career path, keep Christ at the center of your life to satisfy your purpose and fulfillment in life.

- Do not underestimate your value and experiences no matter how gigantic an opportunity seems, regardless of your skin color.

- Pay attention to your mental health as you navigate life and seek out therapy to talk through your emotions. Seeking therapy is okay and I encourage it as a resource for healing. My only regret is that I did not do this sooner.

- Racism is real and it does exist. We must learn how to properly navigate a system that has been in place for centuries with wisdom, confidence in ourselves, and truth.

Do not be naïve that this will not impact you in some way.

♦ Trust in your training and who you are.

♦ Surround yourself with people who believe in you and can speak life into you.

♦ Your dreams are possible. It is your responsibility to try, nobody else's.

♦ Take a step today in pursuit of your dreams.

Author Bio

Gina Guillaume, MD (pronounced Gee-Yom) is a passionate Board Certified, family medicine doctor licensed in the State of Oregon born to two amazing Haitian immigrants and was raised on the beautiful island of Grand Bahama, The Bahamas.

Dr. Guillaume is a first-generation college graduate who has overcome many obstacles including being raised in a high-crime neighborhood, low self-esteem, and childhood trauma. She has proven that no matter your age, upbringing, culture, or hardship, you can accomplish your dreams with a faithful God by your side.

More importantly, Dr. Guillaume has a heart for people with a particular interest in Community Medicine. She is a proud graduate of Howard University College of Medicine (HU... You know) and finished her Family Medicine Residency and Community Health Fellowship at Harbor UCLA Medical Center. She graduated college from Barry University and holds a Master in Health Science from Drexel University.

Dr. Guillaume is not only dedicated to seeing patients in practice, but is a strong advocate for their overall mental, physical, and spiritual wellness. She has a profound insight into the history of medical racism and its long-standing effects of poor health outcomes in marginalized communities along with the impact of social determinants of health that keep underserved communities sick. Dr. Guillaume is a strong advocate for health equity, cultural competency, and increasing the number of Black doctors in medicine, and has given numerous talks about health equity calling for change.

Dr. Guillaume is not shy about sharing her life's journey and her steps to overcoming hardship with the masses. She is, indeed an inspiration to many to follow their dreams through faith, tenacity, and hope.

Appendix

Resources for Survivors of Child Sexual Abuse:

Bahamas:

The National Child Abuse Hotline ph. (242) 322 – 2763 is available 24 hours daily including weekends and holidays offered through the Ministry of Social Services & Urban Development

United States:

Darkness to Light:

Darkness to Light offers a toll-free, confidential helpline for children and adults living in the United

States who need local information and resources about sexual abuse (1-866-FOR-LIGHT) and a crisis text line (Text "LIGHT" to 741741.)

RAINN (Rape, Abuse & Incest National Network)

RAINN operates the National Sexual Assault Hotline (800.656.HOPE) and Safe Helpline for the U.S. Department of Defense. RAINN also offers advice if you suspect a child is being harmed.

Stop It Now! USA

Stop It Now! USA works to prevent sexual abuse of children. Their national prevention helpline (1.888.PREVENT) provides free, confidential, and direct support and information to individuals with questions or concerns about child sexual abuse.

Pre-Med Checklist

- ◆ Locate a mentor early to help guide you with your application to medical school (this can be a medical school student, practicing doctor, or pre-med advisor at your school, etc.)

- ◆ For the most up-to-date list of social media accounts and scholarship opportunities for medical school admission, please reach out to the author via email. This list is continually being updated.

- ◆ Take practice tests often while studying for the MCAT.

- ◆ Give the MCAT test your undivided attention - the mean national MCAT score is 511 and the mean national science undergraduate GPA is 3.6 for medical school admissions. [2]

- ◆ Uworld is a great study tool for the MCAT, medical school standardized tests, and Board exams.

- ◆ Look into financial assistance programs when applying to medical schools.

- Ask about scholarship opportunities while you're applying to medical schools at all institutions.
- Visit your school's Career Center to practice mock interviews before the real interview.
- Learn financial literacy as early as possible. Learn how to budget your money early because it will benefit you greatly in the future.
- Shadow practicing physicians to gain medical experience and ask them for a letter of recommendation when applying to medical school.
- Develop a well-rounded lifestyle. Volunteer, build hobbies, participate in mission trips, etc.
- Seek out Mental Health Therapy sooner than later.
- Pray often.

References

1. ESV Study Bible. (2008). Crossway
   Books.
2. Mighty, M. 2022. Eliminating bias from
   medical school admissions.
   https://www.aamc.org/news/eliminating-
   bias-medical-school-admissions

Made in the USA
Monee, IL
28 August 2025

23153150R00105